about the author

Michael Kerr, award-winning international business speaker, humorist, workshop facilitator, and author, has lived in Alberta for close to twenty years. A former communications manager, Michael is now one of North America's leading authorities on how humour can boost morale, lower stress, motivate employees, and create more productive and inspiring workplaces. Michael makes frequent guest appearances on television and radio and is a humour columnist for newspapers and magazines.

Based in Canmore, Alberta, Michael is the author of four books, including *When Do You Let the Animals Out? A Field Guide to Rocky Mountain Humour*, *The Canadian Rockies Guide to Wildlife Watching*, and *You Can't Be Serious! Putting Humor to Work*. You can surf Michael up at www.MikeKerr.com or at www.WhatsSoFunnyAboutAlberta.com, or contact him by email at mike@mikekerr.com.

The Province of Alberta

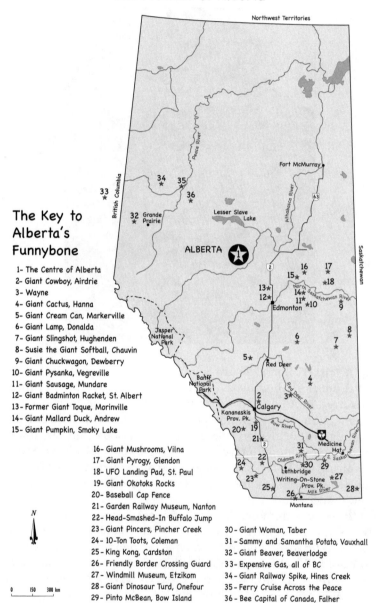

The Key to Alberta's Funnybone

1- The Centre of Alberta
2- Giant Cowboy, Airdrie
3- Wayne
4- Giant Cactus, Hanna
5- Giant Cream Can, Markerville
6- Giant Lamp, Donalda
7- Giant Slingshot, Hughenden
8- Susie the Giant Softball, Chauvin
9- Giant Chuckwagon, Dewberry
10- Giant Pysanka, Vegreville
11- Giant Sausage, Mundare
12- Giant Badminton Racket, St. Albert
13- Former Giant Toque, Morinville
14- Giant Mallard Duck, Andrew
15- Giant Pumpkin, Smoky Lake

16- Giant Mushrooms, Vilna
17- Giant Pyrogy, Glendon
18- UFO Landing Pad, St. Paul
19- Giant Okotoks Rocks
20- Baseball Cap Fence
21- Garden Railway Museum, Nanton
22- Head-Smashed-In Buffalo Jump
23- Giant Pincers, Pincher Creek
24- 10-Ton Toots, Coleman
25- King Kong, Cardston
26- Friendly Border Crossing Guard
27- Windmill Museum, Etzikom
28- Giant Dinosaur Turd, Onefour
29- Pinto McBean, Bow Island

30- Giant Woman, Taber
31- Sammy and Samantha Potato, Vauxhall
32- Giant Beaver, Beaverlodge
33- Expensive Gas, all of BC
34- Giant Railway Spike, Hines Creek
35- Ferry Cruise Across the Peace
36- Bee Capital of Canada, Falher

N

0   150   300 km

what's so <u>funn</u>y about alberta?

michael kerr

FIFTH
HOUSE

Cover design by Paul Shreenan and Reginald Hamilton
Interior design by Cheryl Peddie/Emerge Creative
Interior photographs by Michael Kerr, except pp113 and 114 (Torrington Gopher Hole Museum)
Map by Toby Foord
Edited by Lori Burwash
Copyedited by Terry McIntyre
Proofread by Lesley Reynolds
Scans by ABL Imaging

The publisher gratefully acknowledges the support of The Canada Council for the Arts and the Department of Canadian Heritage.

Canada Council
for the Arts

Conseil des Arts
du Canada

We acknowledge the financial support of the Government of Canada through the Book Publishing Industry Development Program (BPIDP) for our publishing activities.

Printed in Canada by Friesens
05 06 07 08 09 / 5 4 3 2 1

First published in the United States in 2005 by
Fitzhenry & Whiteside
121 Harvard Avenue, Suite 2
Allston, MA 02134

National Library of Canada Cataloguing in Publication Data

Library and Archives Canada Cataloguing in Publication
Kerr, Michael, 1962-
        What's so funny about Alberta? / Michael Kerr.
ISBN 1-894856-32-5
        1. Alberta—Humor. 2. Alberta—Miscellanea. I. Title.
FC3661.3.K47 2005   971.23   C2005-900640-4

Fifth House Ltd.
A Fitzhenry & Whiteside Company
1511, 1800-4 St. SW
Calgary, Alberta T2S 2S5
1-800-387-9776
www.fitzhenry.ca

contents

acknowledgements

Many authors have commented on how creating a book is like giving birth to child. And as with the birthing process, no one could do this alone, especially me, since I'm a man. So a few thanks are in order.

I would like to first thank the many Alberta folks out there on my travels who took the time to chat with me, share some funny thoughts and point me in the right direction, or sometimes the left direction.

To the many folks who entered the "Alberta Laughs" contest I co-hosted on CBC radio, many thanks for your hilarious and creative contributions. Sadly, because I am far too verbose and because there proved to be just too many things funny about Alberta, we (actually it's entirely my publisher's fault, if you must know the truth) had to lop off large chunks of the book, including your witty contributions. If we ever create a volume two (and you can do your part toward that end by going out right now and purchasing more copies of this book), I will do my best to include your wonderful ideas.

I'd like to thank my many friends who are always there to support me during these epic writing adventures, and yes, even those of you who said, "You're doing *what? Why?*"

Charlene Dobmeier and the wonderful people at Fifth House Publishers, of course, deserve my most heartfelt gratitude for steering this baby (see how I've made at least a half-hearted attempt to return to the opening metaphor?) in the right direction. In addition, a huge thanks to Lori Burwash for her masterful editing job and to the ridiculously-easy-to-work-with managing editor Meaghan Craven, for her deft ability to bring the baby all the way home, safe and sound.

As always, I'd like to thank my wife, Claudine, for her unwavering love, support, and encouragement, especially when I made her travel to places to which she really didn't want to go.

And lastly, I'd like to think my parents, Donna and Hugh Kerr, who, as true-blue British Columbians, still accept me into their home—even though I defected to Alberta. This book is dedicated to them.

"Those people out there are different."

—Prime Minister Jean Chrétien commenting on Albertans before the 2000 election

welcome to alberta

Alberta. Wild Rose Country. The princess province. Saskatchewan with mountains. British Columbia with prairies. Texas of the north. The province home to the most number of Albertans.

Let's begin our strange and bewildering journey through the windswept wilds of Alberta with a thorough and rather pointless review of the basics.

Alberta is Canada's second largest province (if you ignore Ontario and Quebec, which, let's face it, most Albertans tend to). At last measure (and no, I don't know when Alberta was last measured, but you'd think, with the possibility of expansion due to global warming and all, we'd want to keep a better tab on these things), Alberta sprawled out at a whopping 661,190 square kilometres (for the Albertans, that's 255,285 square miles). To put this in perspective, Alberta is a tad smaller than the state of Texas (please don't tell them or we'll never hear the end of it) and a bit pudgier than France (please tell them at every possible opportunity).

We're shaped ("we" being the province, not the people) rather like a slice of processed cheese with a large chunk bitten out of the lower west corner by a rabid raccoon. (Of course, there are some Albertans I've met who also resemble this description.) Others (and by "others," I mean me) have suggested that if you glance quickly at a map of Alberta, it resembles Bart Simpson's profile. (Go have a look right now, you'll be truly astounded.)

Alberta is bound to the east by Saskatchewan—where most Albertans are born—and to the west by British

Columbia—where most Albertans go to die. Alberta, as you can see, functions primarily as a holding station for adult western Canadians.

We're home to more than three million folks, of all nationalities and races, especially white ones. Oh sure, we've got some landed immigrants from Newfoundland, but your typical Albertan has, as I've already alluded to, simply wandered on over from Saskatchewan, most likely during a blinding snowstorm while out on a beer run.

Alberta has been ruled by the same political party for more than 318 years, an astonishing feat given that the province only turned one hundred years old in 2005. (Okay, okay, just to demonstrate that I'm not a complete doofus: before the Progressive Conservatives, there was Social Credit and before Social Credit, the United Farmers of Alberta and before them, the Liberals and before the Liberals, assorted Aboriginal tribes and before them, the dinosaurs. Wow, look at that—we've come full circle.) This quaint tradition of re-electing the same party over and over ensures that election results are known well in advance of the opening of the polls, which tends to speed up the entire electoral process, while generating about as much excitement as one might find at a turnip festival.

The capital of Alberta is Edmonton—Canada's most northerly provincial capital—a fact that some Edmontonians brag about, though it's difficult for most Canadians to hear them, what with their voices getting lost in the minus forty degree Arctic winds and all.

Alberta, as an idea and as a landscape, conjures up a lot of imagery, some of it even accurate: Oil. Oil wells. Cows. Cowboys. Cowtown. Calgary. Joe Clark. Vast empty spaces. King Ralph. Natural gas. West Edmonton Mall. Preston Manning. Gophers. The Canadian Rockies. Banff. Jasper. Elk. Tourists. Tourists treed by elk. Giant pyrogies. Ranchers. Ian Tyson. The Calgary Stampede. Stampede Wrestling. UFO landing pads. Stockwell Day. Dinosaurs. Grizzlies. Wheat. The Badlands. Rodeos. Flames vs. Oilers. Wayne Gretzky and Jerome Iginla. "The Hat." Pronghorns. Farmers. Peace River Country. k.d. lang. Alberta beef. The foothills. Athabasca River. Mike from Canmore. The Columbia Icefields. Jann Arden. Chinook winds. Waterton Lakes. Did I mention cowboys already? How about oil?

Cows, I mean, surely I mentioned cows?

And now, after that whirlwind of imagery, allow me to wax poetic about Alberta for a moment or two . . .

. . . Okay, enough waxing, let's just get on with it, shall we? After all, Albertans are not known for their waxing abilities. We tend to be more of a "let's get on with it" kind of people. And I am, after all, an Albertan.

Being an Albertan is not something I gloat about (unless you happen to hail from Ontario). Nor am I ashamed of the label, as some easterners apparently believe I should feel. I simply know it to be true, not because of any stirring in my heart when I smell cow manure, nor because I get misty-eyed every time I hear "Alberta Bound" on the radio, but merely because my driver's licence tells me so. It's right there on the upper left-hand corner—you really can't miss it.

Now, in the interest of full disclosure, allow me to confess something—I am not a *native* Albertan. Surprisingly, I don't hail from Saskatchewan, but from British Columbia. And while growing up in "Supernatural British Columbia," I knew only one thing about Albertans: they were the world's worst drivers. The running joke in BC was that the old yellow Alberta licence plates were really learner plates, and that Albertans were horrific drivers when travelling through mountainous and curvaceous British Columbia because the flatlanders from Alberta drove in straight lines only. All this I learned from my father, who evidently had issues with Albertans. (Incidentally, I've now come to appreciate just what a ridiculous assertion this is—*everyone* knows that Saskatchewan drivers are the worst.)

Later, as a teenager, I learned that Alberta represented the Holy Grail, the promised land, a very cool place, for two important reasons:

1. You can get your learner's driver's licence when you are only fourteen years old.
2. In Alberta you can legally drink alcohol upon turning eighteen.

These two laws not only lure thousands of unsuspecting Saskatchewan teenagers to Alberta each year, I think they also make a valid case for declaring Alberta a distinct society within Canada, far more distinct than Quebec could ever dream of being (especially when you toss Myron Thompson and Mike from Canmore in for good measure).

Now, as a more mature and wildly handsome adult, I realize that these are rather frightening laws. (Here's an interesting little fact to chew on the next time you pull onto Calgary's Deerfoot Trail: most fourteen-year-olds can't see over the friggin' steering wheel!)

Fortunately, there is one critical aspect of Alberta life that overrides any concern over laws such as these. And that defining Albertan fact, as Albertan as Ralph Klein's underwear, as Albertan as Wayne Gretzky-before-Peter Pocklington-stabbed-us-all-in-our-collective-hearts-and-ripped-out-our-souls-by-selling-Wayne-to-the-United States, as Albertan as Ian Tyson and k.d. lang riding together buck naked and eating beef atop a bighorn sheep on the open range in the middle of a hailstorm, is this: Alberta has no provincial sales tax.

That's right. Nada. Zippo percent. Really, it's this one crucial aspect of Albertan life that makes every Albertan, deep down to the bottom of our oil wells, truly proud to be an Albertan. Every time we purchase something, our Albertan hearts swell with Albertan pride as we wait for the sound of the extra chime of the cash register . . . and wait . . . and wait some more . . . and then giggle maniacally out of the store counting our hard-earned Albertan pennies.

"No sales tax" has become our mantra. Our calling card. Our reason for existence. Our reason for shopping. It really ought to be our official motto: "Alberta: We Don't Pay No Stinkin' Sales Tax!"

Heck, even Alberta's official motto—"Strong and Free"—is obviously a not-so-veiled reference to our absence of provincial sales tax. In fact, what's the first thing any true Albertan says to any *non-Albertan* Canadian? That's right—we throw our no-sales-tax way of life giddily into their non-Albertan faces faster than you can say "GST."

According to one study I made up, provincial sales tax comes up in conversations with Albertans more often than the weather (which, for Canadians, really is an astounding statistic, especially if it was true). Here's a typical exchange I overheard on a recent flight to Toronto:

Non-Albertan: "So where are you from?"
Albertan: "Alberta. We don't have a provincial sales tax."

Non-Albertan: "Um, yeah I know."

Albertan: "No, really, it's nothing. It's 0 percent. Like when you go to the cash register and buy something, they don't add anything on, unless you count that goddamn, archaic, money-grabbing, regressive, economically stifling GST devised by eastern politicians who are out to ruin us."

Non-Albertan: "Right. I'd like to sleep now."

Albertan: "Where are you from? I bet wherever it is, you pay a sales tax, don't you?"

Non-Albertan: "I'm from Newfoundland."

Albertan (after the laughter subsides): "Holy mother-of-pearl—Newfoundland? Your sales tax is like 87 percent, isn't it? Holy sweet Joseph and Mary. You know, we don't pay any provincial sales tax in Alberta. Nothing."

Of course, not all the conversations go like this. Sometimes the other person is from Toronto.

So there you have it—Alberta in a nutshell. This insightful introduction ought to provide you with more than enough background material to truly enjoy this book, or complete your master's thesis.

Of course, there is *so* much more to Alberta than our absence of sales tax. For instance, we also have one of the lowest provincial income tax rates. And don't even get me started on the small business tax. Believe it or not, there's even *more* to Alberta than dead dinosaurs and low taxes. And I went in search of it.

Yes, I criss-crossed this gigantic province in search of the *real* Alberta. And if not quite the real Alberta, then at the very least in search of things I could make up about Alberta. Most importantly, I sought out things we could all share a hearty, wheat-encrusted Albertan laugh over. Like my first book, *When Do You Let the Animals Out? A Field Guide to Rocky Mountain Humour* (that you really should rush out and buy for reference, especially in Alberta, because you won't have to pay any provincial sales tax), this book attempts to seek out the true underbelly of our home, home on the range, through intensive investigative journalism and exhaustive research, and by making things up as I go along.

Sure, this tends to blur the line between fact and fiction, but since when has that stopped any good journalist?

So with my trusty tape recorder, laptop, and complete collection of Ian Tyson, Nickelback, and Jann Arden CDs in tow (they're Albertan, you know), I shopped 'til I dropped at West Edmonton Mall, hunted down Trekkies in Vulcan, and unearthed the real truth as to how Alberta maintains its much coveted rat-free status. I gazed hungrily in stunned awe at the world's largest pyrogy, looked for signs of extraterrestrials at the St. Paul UFO landing pad, and wandered the streets of Banff in search of a national park.

I interviewed thousands of Albertans, and if not thousands, at least seven or so, posing such penetrating, hard-hitting questions as: What makes an Albertan an Albertan? What's a real Albertan, and how can you spot the fakes? Is "Alberta culture" really an oxymoron? How many Albertans does it take to screw in a light bulb? What, besides federal government policies, do Albertans find funny? Where the hell am I, and how can I get back on to the main highway from here?

Above all else, I went in search of an answer to the ultimate Alberta question, a question once posed to me by a somewhat befuddled American tourist in Banff who wanted to know "Where does Alberta end and Canada begin?"

If that isn't a question worthy of some weighty Canadian constitutional navel-gazing, I don't know what is.

I hope you enjoy the book. If you take offence at anything I've written about Alberta or your particular home town, please, by all means, make like a true-blue Albertan and write to your Member of Parliament in Ottawa, because if you're a *real* Albertan, you know that, ultimately, *they* are the ones to blame.

i'm mike, from canmore

As your intrepid guide to the wackier side of Alberta, please allow me to properly introduce myself. I'm Mike . . . from Canmore.

Now, before you get all excited, no, I'm not the dimwitted, duller-than-an-unglazed-doughnut, Calgary Flames baseball cap–wearing, CBC *Royal Canadian Air Farce* character "Mike from Canmore." But I am Mike. And I *really* am from Canmore.

As another Mike from Canmore, I've always felt a certain affinity toward the real Mike from Canmore, even though the "real" Mike from Canmore isn't really from Canmore, nor is he a Mike. Mike from Canmore was played by the brilliantly goofy late John Morgan, originally from Wales. So, technically speaking, that makes me a more real Mike from Canmore than the real Mike from Canmore could ever really hope to be.

Really. I mean, I actually live in Canmore. And my name's Mike. So I really am Mike from Canmore. The other Mike from Canmore is a fake. Except of course, there wouldn't *be* a "Mike from Canmore" if it wasn't for the fake Mike from Canmore who claimed to be Mike from Canmore and therefore is known as the "real" Mike from Canmore. This can lead to a bit of confusion from time to time. (And if this sounds like a segue into a story, then, by gosh, you're absolutely right.)

Take the time, for example, I was preparing for a conference keynote address at a Canmore hotel. One of my audience members stealthily approached me at the front of the room and discreetly slid a few postcards under my nose.

"Could you sign these please?" the man politely asked.

"Huh?" I so eloquently responded.

"Could you please autograph these? My family would kill me if I didn't get your autograph."

"Huh?" I repeated—only this time I scrunched up my face and tilted my head in a quizzical doglike manner to emphasize my sheer and utter bafflement.

"Your autograph, we'd really like your autograph," he repeated, beginning to take on the tone of someone who is speaking to a person who is obviously either a little hard of hearing or just plain daft.

"Your family wants *my* autograph?" I asked, my tone betraying a certain something, although I'm not sure what.

"Yes. And your dog's too!"

"My dog?"

"Yes, of course!" he said enthusiastically.

"My dog?" I repeated.

"Yes, yes, you know—Norm."

Then, out of nowhere, the bulb lit up so brightly atop my head I was afraid I was going to blind the poor fellow.

"Ahhhhhhhh," I said slowly, as if readying for a throat swab, "you think I'm Mike from Canmore. *That* Mike from Canmore. The *real* Mike from Canmore."

"You mean you're not?"

"No."

"But our information sheet says your name is Mike."

"It is."

"And it says you're from Canmore."

"I am."

"Then you're Mike from Canmore!" he said, his face lighting up as if he had just solved the crime of the century.

"Well, I am indeed *a* Mike from Canmore, but I'm not *the* Mike from Canmore who you and your family want an autograph from. I'm just Mike from Canmore. Not, you know, 'Mike from Canmore.'" (I actually said this while gesturing the quotation marks with my fingers.)

"Oh," he replied, his face now dimming several notches. Then, after a moment of deep contemplation, his face relit like a Christmas tree on Viagra. (It really was a tad unnerving, as though someone was playing with a dimmer switch inside his forehead.)

"But you are *a* Mike from Canmore?" he asked cautiously.

"Yes, well, yes. There are dozens, perhaps hundreds of

Mikes from Canmore, and, yes, I am one of them. I guess I *am* Mike from Canmore," I said confidently, as though I had just been bestowed with the Nobel Peace Prize. I'd never been more proud of my name and community as I was at that very moment.

"You know . . . my family will never know the difference," the man started slowly. "I mean, you are Mike from Canmore, but they don't need to know that you're not *Mike* from Canmore. Besides, now that I think about it, you actually are the *real* Mike from Canmore."

"Well, not really," I replied. "Although I am Mike from Canmore. Just not, you know, 'Mike from Canmore.'"

"Right, but you *are* Mike from Canmore."

"Um, yeah, I guess."

"So just autograph the damn postcards so I can get the hell out of here."

"Well, okay," I replied, feeling a little naughty as I scrawled "Greetings from Mike from Canmore" across the back of the postcard, wondering if I could be charged with impersonating a national dork.

Although it wasn't the last time I've been confused with someone famous (although usually it's the kid who played Danny on the *Partridge Family*, Anne Murray, or Tom Cruise), it was certainly one of the most memorable times.

Ever since that day, I've thought about convincing the Canmore town council to declare an official Mike from Canmore holiday in honour of Canmore's greatest ambassador. There could be a Mike from Canmore parade with all the baseball-capped Mikes marching dopily in unison, a giant Mike from Canmore sculpture erected at the town entrance, and an "Open Mike" night at the local bars, where all the Mikes would drink and eat for free (this, naturally, being the best part of my master plan).

Until that wonderful day arrives, I'm Mike from Canmore, too, signing off.

?

Mike from Canmore began as Mike from Pickering. Can you even imagine "Mike from Pickering"? It just sounds so ridiculously unfunny, anti-Albertan, and, frankly, a little lame, doesn't it? I mean, whoever thought up Mike from Pickering probably also thought up the GST and the National Energy Program.

Mike from Pickering was a dimwitted fellow calling in on a radio talk show spoof by the Royal Canadian Air Farce. The 1991 segment was taped in front of a studio audience in Scarborough, Ontario, where, evidently, "Mike from Pickering" would have incited much jocularity. However, the radio segment never aired.

Later that year, the Air Farce resurrected the sketch while recording a show in Banff. This time, they referred to the caller as Mike from Canmore, knowing that Mike from Pickering wouldn't have the same goofy resonance in Alberta. Whenever the radio host of the fictional station COW-FM asked the caller a question, John Morgan repeated his reply, "I'm Mike, from Canmore." The segment made it to the airwaves—thus, Mike from Canmore was born.

An Albertan was touring Paris when he came upon the Eiffel Tower. He turns to a local and says, "Wow, that's impressive. How many barrels a day do you get from that?"

———————

It was recently revealed that automobiles have been secretly outfitted with black boxes, similar to those found in airplanes, to document the last moments before a fatal collision.

The results from three years' worth of data show that in all provinces, with one exception, the final words of 85 percent of the drivers were "Oh damn!"

The one exception was Alberta, where the last words of 90 percent of the drivers were "Hold my beer and watch this!"

———————

How many Albertans does it take to change a light bulb?
Ten. One to change the bulb and nine to complain about the National Energy Program.

top ten ways to become an albertan

For those Albertan residents silly enough to be born outside of Alberta, there are still some ways you can become an Albertan. I mean, a real Albertan. You see, simply moving to Alberta won't cut it. Unless you've lived here for at least eighty years, you'll always be considered from afar: an easterner, a Newfie, or—worst of the lot—a Roughriders fan.

So if you've demonstrated unusually poor judgment by being born out-of-province, like myself, I'm happy to share the following shortcuts that can speed up the assimilation process on the road to full-fledged Albertanhood. Please keep in mind, however, that carrying out merely one or two of these recommendations won't, as we say in Alberta, slice the beef. You should probably plan to complete at least seven of the ten. But be forewarned: even then you may be looked upon with a certain degree of suspicion.

Mike's "Ten steps to becoming an Albertan" program

10. **Publicly denounce the province/nation of your birth.**
    This may involve holding a "Why Saskatchewan Sucks" party, or it may be as simple as taking up arms against your former birthplace.

9. **Write a letter to the editor denouncing the Liberals' National Energy Program of the early 1980s.**
    Sure, it happened more than twenty years ago, but your letter will eloquently point out that if it happened once, it could happen again, only next time the Feds will be com-

ing for our children and womenfolk.

8. Replace all your vehicles with pickup trucks.
This is particularly important if you're currently driving a wimpy vehicle such as a Honda Civic, SUV, or Hummer.

7. Eat beef. Lots of beef.
Put beef in your milkshakes, feed your gerbils beef, and sleep with some ground beef under your pillow. Consider giving beef away as a thoughtful Christmas present, or use a slab of Grade A Alberta beef to say "I love you" to that special someone on Valentine's Day. For bonus points, plan to have the popular "I Love Alberta Beef" bumper sticker tattooed to your ass.

6. Know thy enemy.
Create your own "Top Ten Reasons Edmonton Sucks" list for use in Calgary and a "Top Ten Reasons Calgary Sucks" list for use in Edmonton. This advice might just save your life.

5. Visit Banff, but don't be too happy about it.
Stroll around like you own the joint, then, when back at home and people ask if you ever go to Banff, look at them as though you have just inhaled a can of insecticide and inform them, "I *never* go to Banff. It's too crowded, too expensive, and overrun with tourists. That's why I only go to Kananaskis Country for my camping vacations."

4. Drive like an Albertan.
Drive from Edmonton to Calgary (or vice versa) in under two hours . . . in the winter . . . during a blinding snowstorm . . . without snow tires . . . after they've closed the highway even to snowplows. The rest of the year, simply try to ignore annoying distractions such as yellow lights, speed limit signs, or other drivers.

3. Memorize the Alberta Advantage Pledge.
This involves memorizing a lengthy list of all the advantages of living in Alberta. This will take months of hard study, as the list currently tops three thousand items.

Start slowly, by familiarizing yourself with the top bene-fits: No provincial sales tax, no rats, lots of sunshine, lots of oil, the Rocky Mountains, Alberta beef, lots of neat old dinosaur bones, and, um, oh yeah, no provincial sales tax. Repeat to out-of-province guests over and over as necessary.

2. **Lift a mug with Ralph.**

Tell folks as often as possible that you once drank a beer with Ralph Klein at the old St. Louis Tavern in Calgary. (It doesn't matter that you never actually did this, because neither did the tens of thousands of other Albertans who claim to have done this at one time or another.)

1. **Deport a rat.**

Alberta, as we'll see shortly, is very proud of its rat-free status, so if you want to earn heartfelt accolades from Albertans, hunt down and deport an illegal rat. Sure, it could take decades to actually find a rat in Alberta, but do you want to stay here or not?

my most albertan moment

It was the ninth of August, 1988. A date that carries some rather weighty significance if you're an Albertan . . .

My girlfriend and I were in my pickup truck in the middle of southern Alberta. I'd like to be able to tell you where, but I can't because we were lost, and not being able to tell folks where you are comes with the whole "being lost" thing. All I know is that we were somewhere east of Calgary and north of Mexico.

We (okay "I," although in fairness, my girlfriend *was* the designated navigator) had taken several wrong turns, ending up on a gravel road in the middle of nowhere, smack dab in the centre of nothing, somewhere between anywhere and nowhere—which basically describes much of Alberta. Despite my maleness, I would have gladly asked for directions, had there been someone to ask. Alas, there was no one. We could have been at a travel agency in North Korea and had more options for asking directions. But here, in southern Alberta, it was just us, a few trillion acres of farmers' fields, and a couple of gophers that, for the sake of argument, we'll call Hal and Ethel.

I remember looking around, recalling those old "the prairies are so flat you can watch your dog run away for three weeks" jokes and thinking to myself, "We're not in Kansas anymore, Toto." It was hot, dusty, and oh-so-flat. For the first time since moving to Alberta, I felt like a true Albertan. I mean heck-gosh-darn-it, there I was sitting out in the open prairie in a pickup truck, listening to a country music station complete with a coyote-sounding cowboy wailing about how he was "lost in the middle of a field of heartache." Much the way we were.

Then it happened. Through the static, amid the flowing wheat, the song was abruptly interrupted with Alberta's announcement of the year. It was one of those pivotal moments in Alberta history. One that you forevermore remember what you were doing, who you were doing it to, and where you were doing it (unless, of course, you were lost) when it happened.

Wayne Gretzky had just been traded.

Sold down the river to the Los Angeles Kings like a sack of Taber corn. Packaged up in a box and handed away like a snack pack of Tim Hortons Timbits. Expunged from our borders faster than a Saskatchewan rat.

We were aghast! We felt betrayed! Confused! Bewildered! And not just because the radio station went back to the country song. No, we felt betrayed because this was our Wayne they were talking about. Sure, he could be a whiny little pain in the ass sometimes, but he was *our* whiny little pain in the ass. And no, he wasn't a native Albertan, but by golly he had been adopted by Alberta at an age when most adoptive parents wouldn't even dream of adoption. He had grown up in front of our very eyes. He had given us all a reason to go to Edmonton. Above all else, Wayne had helped bring the Stanley Cup to Alberta for the very first time, keeping it out of the hands of those eastern National Energy Program–loving bastards.

If we were lost *before* the announcement, you can imagine how lost we now felt. Even Hal and Ethel (if you'll recall, the two gophers I spoke highly of earlier) seemed slightly stunned.

Brokenhearted, my girlfriend began to sob. She had lost her Wayne. Plus, she was lost in the middle of Alberta with me (which, as it turns out, was the *real* reason she was sobbing).

We bid adieu to Hal and Ethel, started up the truck, and drove on down the dusty gravel road in silence. We needn't talk. Both of us knew what the other was thinking: Without Wayne, what will become of the Edmonton Oilers? Of Alberta? What will happen to Canadian hockey? And where the hell *are* we?

After ten minutes of silent contemplation, we encountered a farmer heading in our direction in a pickup truck. We both slowed to a standstill and rolled down our windows.

"Howdy," I said, trying to sound more Albertan than I really was at the time.

"Howdy yourself," he replied. "Did you hear about Gretzky?"

"Yup," I said, nodding solemnly.

The farmer's face exploded into an enormous grin. "Never did like that little gaffer. Me, I'm a Calgary Flames fan through and through. This is the happiest day of my life!"

It was then that it hit me: I was experiencing a truly Albertan moment, my most Albertan moment to date. After all, there I was sitting in a pickup truck, in the middle of a farmer's field, talking to a real Albertan farmer about one of our defining Albertan characteristics—our deep respect and/or hatred for the Edmonton Oilers and/or Calgary Flames—only moments after hearing the hockey announcement of the century.

The kind gentleman then directed us back onto a main highway, which wasn't so much a main highway as a bumpy dirt road that would eventually lead to a narrow gravel road that would intersect with another gravel road that would get us to within ten miles of an almost secondary highway.

Despite the heat, the dust, the endless drive, and the bumps along the way, we knew it could have been worse. *We* could have been traded out of Alberta to Los Angeles.

As we drove under a glorious prairie sunset, that was a fate neither of us wished upon anyone.

my most canadian moment, in alberta

B anff, Alberta, is, for me, the quintessential Canadian town. Banff, after all, plays host to the entire world. As such, it serves as a sort of international ambassador of Alberta.

It's more than just that. Set within Canada's first and most treasured national park, surrounded by rugged, snowcapped peaks, lush forests, and hordes of tour buses, Banff just *feels* Canadian. It is the sort of place where, after spending only a few days, you feel like dressing up like a Mountie, jumping on a moose, and chasing beavers all day. It's just *that* Canadian.

So it seems rather fitting that my "most Canadian moment" occurred when I was living in Banff. It was a cool autumn day. The leaves were blushing with fall colour, and the air was rich with the sound of Banff's infamous urban elk, as the bull elk serenaded tourists and cow elk alike with their haunting bugles.

I was on my way home from the grocery store when I encountered one of these urban bull elk standing defiantly in someone's front yard. The park paparazzi (a.k.a. park tourists) had completely engulfed the enormous bull. Cameras were whirring and flashing. People were giggling, gawking, posing, and pointing.

This was a natural reaction to spotting an elk in Banff. After all, this is what folks had paid their money for. Unfortunately, these photo ops tend to be extremely dangerous, for both elk and paparazzi alike. But just as the elk began to demonstrate telltale signs of aggression (including ear flapping, lip curling, and kicking people in the head), a park warden arrived.

This, dear reader, is where my most Canadian moment began.

The warden got out of his truck and, it being a rather cool day, pulled out Canada's greatest contribution to the fashion world—a toque—and placed it snugly on his head. This wasn't just any old toque. This particular toque was adorned with a large red maple leaf. I recall looking at him and thinking, "How very Canadian of him."

The park warden then went to the back of his warden truck and pulled out the elk motivational weapon of choice—a hockey stick. The stick had a yellow plastic litter bag placed over the blade like a loose-fitting condom. Now, appropriately armed, the park warden broke through the crowd and, like an Edmonton Oiler on a breakaway (this was back when they actually had breakaways), tore after the elk, waving the stick back and forth high above his head while screaming like a chimpanzee on uppers.

Watching this bizarre scene unfold, I remember thinking to myself, "Does it *get* more Canadian than this?" After all, here was a guy wearing a maple leaf–emblazoned toque, chasing a wild animal out of a yard . . . with a hockey stick. The only way it could have been more Canadian was if he'd been drinking a can of beer and chewing on a slab of back bacon.

Naturally, the American tourists in the crowd were eating this up: "I told you this is what they do in Canada, Marge—they chase after the wild animals with their hockey sticks!"

On cue, appropriately freaked out by the stick-brandishing maniac, the elk bolted from the mayhem. The paparazzi quickly dispersed. And the oh-so-Canadian warden left.

I stood alone on the sidewalk for a moment, pondering what had just happened, somehow feeling a wee bit more Canadian than I had when I woke up that morning.

land of the giants

In Alberta, size really does matter.

Albertans like to think big. And in a Texan sort of way, we're proud of our bigness. We've got big mountains, big open ranges, big rivers, big glaciers, big ranches, big sky, big dinosaurs, big cows, big outdoor shows, big towers, big malls, the world's biggest dump trucks, bigger-than-life politicians, and a honkin' big Easter egg.

To help gain an understanding of this almost compulsive obsession with size, I went in search of some of the lesser-known Albertan giants on a little road trip that me and my homey (also known as my lovely spouse) dubbed the Albertan Giants Road Tour. (We're hoping to release an album by the same name early next year.)

Our pursuit for the giants of Alberta would lead us on a circuitous route north of Calgary, through the centre of the province, criss-crossing our way as far north as Lac La Biche, as far east as the Saskatchewan border, with approximately a gazillion and one stops in between (mostly for pee breaks, mind you). We were going to put a lot of miles on the old Honda, which meant one thing and one thing only. That's right, we needed to stock up on doughnuts. (My wife failed to see the logic as well, but that didn't stop me.)

Our first stop was Airdrie, where I really wanted to get a photograph of the giant cowboy that stands like a giant cowboy beacon just east off Highway 2. Specifically, I wanted to get a photo of the giant cowboy's crotch. Why? I'm not sure. Perhaps I have issues.

"That's really, really childish," my wife said after I told her of my plan.

"I know, that's why I'm doing it," I responded.

Mission accomplished, we headed east for the Alberta Badlands and Drumheller, "The Dinosaur Capital of Canada"— a place where big has ruled the landscape for a long time.

Our route to Drumheller took us along Highway 9, past the roadside statue of Squirt the Skunk at Beiseker, and also past a sign that warned motorists of low-flying aircraft, causing me to wonder just how low these planes are flying that I, an earth-bound motorist, had to be worried about them. My god, there are enough idiots on the road without having to worry about wayward pilots forgetting to turn off their signal light.

Horseshoe Canyon, just a few minutes west of Drumheller, offers the perfect primer stop for anyone new to the

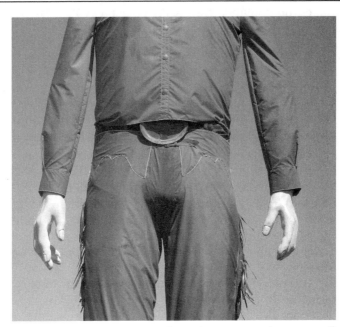

"The biggest crotch in the west."

Badlands, revealing the first hint that the landscape is about to dramatically change. It looks very much like a small-scale version of a canyon you'd expect to find in the Utah desert, only without Mormons. It's not hard to imagine, looking down at this stunning vista, that dinosaurs once ruled this corner of the planet.

Which reminds me. A little back story for you before we head on into Drumheller. Alberta once teemed with dinosaurs. Fast forward to the twenty-first century and you're pretty much caught up. Who said history had to be boring?

The fact that dinosaurs once reigned supreme here makes me wonder if it could be that Albertans were, in some cosmic sort of way, predestined to be obsessed about size. Or perhaps in our quest for hugeness, we're still trying to make up for the fact that we killed off the last of the dinosaurs? (Now, I know that technically we didn't kill them off, but that could just be a mere technicality. You see it in murder cases all the time these days.)

Dropping below the surface of the prairie landscape into the depths of the Badlands, you really do get a sense of travelling back in time—it helped that the radio was playing an old Elvis song. As you draw closer to Drumheller, it almost feels as though at any time a *Tyrannosaurus rex* could run across the highway—wouldn't *that* make for a nasty bit of road kill?

We turned south to the small town of Rosedale, where we'd be setting up camp for the night. Friends joined us for a pleasant evening around the campfire, save for the fact that one of these friends enjoys singing his own made-up country songs. If you have friends like this, try to replace them immediately.

The next morning welcomed us into her Alberta bosom with a brilliant blue sky. We ventured first to the famous Rosedale suspension bridge. The entrance sign to Rosedale had said "Home of the Suspension Bridge," making it sound as though Rosedale had invented the darn thing, so we figured it was a must-see.

The 117-metre-long bridge spans the Red Deer River on the eastern edge of town. Given that it was a windy day, crossing the footbridge gave the impression that we were all still very, very drunk, when in fact only one of us was still drunk.

A sign let us know that this bridge was a provincial historical site. (You know what I'd like to see on just one historical site sign? A sign that simply reads "This sign is very, very old.")

Driving through Rosedale, we noticed that a few residents had painted their garage doors with dinosaurs and that the fence surrounding the baseball field was particularly massive. I suggested it was to help keep the dinosaurs at bay.

Cruising the ten-minute drive north along the Hoo Doo Trail to Drumheller, we tuned into the tourist information station, which proved to be light on information, heavy on coma-inducing music. In fact, I'm almost certain the music they were playing predates the dinosaurs.

Although it would have been nice to see the locals dressed up like cave people, it's clear that Drumheller has embraced its dino theme in a dino-mite way. There was the Hoo Doo Motel, the Jurassic Best Western Inn, the Fred and Barney Restaurant, cute cutouts of cavemen and dinosaurs on most light posts, a *Tyrannosaurus rex* head bursting through the wall of the local IGA grocery store, and—looming in the distance—the threatening head of a T. Rex towering over the town. In addition, the flags were at half-mast, which I thought

was a rather nice way to honour the death of the dinosaurs.

The entire town is also littered with cartoon-like, very friendly-looking green, purple, pink, and even polka-dotted dinosaur statues. The fire station features the little-known Dalmatian dinosaur, while the Royal Canadian Legion is home to a green *Triceratops* right next to the "Lest We Forget" memorial—making it seem as though it's the fallen dinosaurs being honoured.

The star attraction in town, though, is the big guy himself: the giant T. Rex that, from our vantage point downtown, towered above the

local drug store. It was very surreal looking. I half expected to see a throng of Japanese tourists fleeing the city.

Strolling over to the information site and home of the "World's Largest Dinosaur," the first thing we noticed was a Calgary Flames flag sticking out of the giant lizard's mouth—giving the appearance that the dinosaur was breathing fire or, more believably, had just swallowed a Flames fan that had somehow pissed him off.

This particular T. Rex weighs in at more than 65,000 kilograms and stands 25 metres, or eight storeys, tall, making it about four times the actual size of a real-live T. Rex, which of course is a silly comparison since there are no real-live T. Rexes anymore.

"You know what would help this attraction be more interactive? If the dinosaur passed gas every hour on the hour." My helpful suggestion only drew confused looks from the tourists around me. Evidently, they liked their attractions to remain quiet and odour-free.

Unlike most giant attractions, this one allows you to walk up inside it, into the dinosaur's mouth. It costs three dollars to clamber up the 106 steps, roughly three cents per stair. Along the way, there are fossils imprinted in the walls, and sound effects that, oddly enough, do not include burping or farting. It is very dark and eerie at a few spots, making it the perfect place to make small children cry (not that I would ever do that).

Few people realize just how friendly the dinosaurs really were.

Here, as we climbed through the bowels of the beast, I thought of yet another helpful idea. We all know that T. Rexes were voracious meat eaters, so a nice, realistic touch would be to include some rotting animal flesh on the climb up. "Just an idea."

Standing in the dinosaur's lower jaw, peering out over its massive teeth, I had an impressive view of the area and, more importantly, a chance to see if anyone was breaking into my vehicle. Jumping up and down caused the entire head to move, as though it was going to devour us at any moment. Since my wife has an unnatural fear of being eaten by dinosaurs, we quickly retreated out of the mouth and down the stairs.

Back on terra firma, we bid adieu to the World's Largest Dinosaur and headed for the world-famous Royal Tyrrell Museum. Named for dinosaur hunter Joseph B. Tyrrell, the museum is a world-class facility. You can easily spend a day strolling through the exhibits and exploring the surrounding Badlands. There are even dinosaur field digs offering you and your family (or, if you prefer, someone else's family) the chance to get down and dirty out in the field.

In addition to the numerous displays, the museum lets you watch real paleontologists at work in their labs, something a lot of professions don't offer. I mean, have you ever seen a facility where you can watch accountants working?

There was a great display featuring a sabre-toothed tiger. He must have been really, really old, though, because he looked a little "long in the tooth." (Neanderthals probably told that joke all the time.)

You can meet our own dinosaur namesakes here, too, which, being Alberta, we of course have. Three in fact. *Albertosaurus* is described as 8 metres of fearsome carnivore, a hunter possessing greater speed and agility than the rather wimpy and socially awkward *Tyrannosaurus rex. Edmontonia* was a smaller armoured dinosaur with small feet and weak jaws, while *Edmontosaurus* was a plant-eating duck-billed dinosaur sporting a fleshy crest along its back and tail.

After losing yourself in the fascinating exhibits for several hours, visitors end up, amazingly enough, by some bizarre fluke of design, in the gift shop, where one can spend a small fortune on dinosaur paraphernalia.

Upon spending three hours in the museum and climbing inside the giant T. Rex, I certainly saw how Albertans could become obsessed about size.

The daring author was nearly crushed by a passing T. Rex.

?

silly tourist questions from drumheller

Where do you keep the real dinosaurs?

Does pee fossilize?

If you find the bones underground, doesn't that mean the dinosaurs lived underground?

Are there dinosaurs living in places we don't know about?

How do you know the dinosaurs' names?

Would dinosaurs taste like chicken or more like frog legs?

If baby cats are kittens, and baby dogs are puppies, what do you call baby dinosaurs?

Two more stops awaited us before leaving the Badlands. The first was a side trip to the former mining town of Wayne. Wayne is nestled in a small valley about 14 kilometres south-west of Drumheller, at the end of a little windy highway that has apparently made it into the *Guinness Book of World Records* for having the most number of bridges (eleven) in the shortest distance (9 kilometres).

In addition to the rustic-looking Last Chance Saloon, Wayne is home to about a dozen homes. I loved the entrance sign: "Welcome to Wayne. Population Then: 2,490, Now 42." That and the "Danger" sign riddled with bullet holes definitely gave the town a western flavour.

Since there were still live human beings making their home in Wayne, it seemed odd that it was listed as a ghost town—unless the people we were seeing were indeed ghosts and not actual human beings, in which case Wayne is definitely a must-see.

Stop number two was north of Drumheller, just past the Tyrrell Museum, where the "World's Smallest Church" reputedly sits. A quick search on the Web reveals that the world's smallest church is also found at Yuma, Arizona; Davenport, Iowa; Warrenton, Texas; Bellevue, Alberta; and approximately seven hundred other locations for your convenience. Anyway, you have to figure that sooner or later the Japanese will have figured out how to get this sucker down to the size of a microchip.

This particular small church stands about 2 metres high

and offers seating for about six folks. I was surprised no one had thought to build a massive dinosaur next to it, terrorizing the churchgoers. Given that this still was officially a place of spiritual sanctity, I guess it made sense to leave it as is.

Since this was the Albertan Giants Road Tour, not the Tour to Visit Little Tiny Things, we needed to head back to the campsite for an early start the following day. Big things were awaiting us.

?

Saying good-bye to our country-music-singing friends, my wife and I made a last-minute call to head way out of our way east, all on your behalf—see what I do for you?—to check out the giant cactus at Hanna.

Hanna, population 2,996, "Proud to be the Home of Nickelback," is also home to a giant grey goose, owing to its status as "Home of the Grey Goose." Past Hanna along Highway 9, we pulled into a truck weigh scale to weigh ourselves and see how much weight we'd lost on the trip so far. After figuring out we'd each gained five pounds, we made a pact to stop weighing ourselves.

The giant cactus sits east of Hanna, at the crossroads of Highways 9 and 36, home of the Partnership Rest Stop. The gas station, Cactus Café, and gigantic green cactus give the isolated place a rather Arizona-like feel—the kind of place you see in movies, a film noir where a handsome drifter (not unlike myself) with a mysterious past (not unlike myself) stops in to use the washroom (again, not unlike myself).

The movie comparison ended when I made my wife pose in front of the enormous metallic cactus, prompting someone in the parking lot to comment that we must be from Saskatchewan (as if Albertans would never partake in such outrageous behaviour?).

Eastwards we pressed. Every car had a Saskatchewan licence plate, including the idiot who nearly clipped us, prompting me to say some not very nice things about Saskatchewan drivers and to conclude that Saskatchewan people are the world's worst drivers. See what just one idiot can do on behalf of an entire province of innocent people?

Stanmore, although we saw it with our own eyes, failed to

appear on our road map. I don't know about you, but being left off a road map would depress the hell out of me.

Before turning north, we popped into Cereal and Oyen, both of which have life-sized pronghorn statues that appear to be exactly the same. Obviously these towns capitalized on a great two-for-one deal on antelopes.

North along Highway 41, then west on Highway 12, our route took us past Consort, Veteran, Throne, and Coronation. These, along with a few other towns following the rail line here, were named to honour the coronation of King George V in 1911.

I stopped at a family rest stop along here and noticed there were condom machines in the washroom. Condoms at a family rest stop? Isn't it a little late?

At Castor, we popped in to look for the beaver statue, but it was missing in action. Worse still, the locals I talked to didn't even seem to have noticed, nor were they the slightest bit distressed about the beaver's absence! Am I the only Albertan who cares about our cultural heritage?

So on we went to Markerville, southwest of Red Deer and home to a giant cream can. As giant cans of cream go, it was very pleasant.

We pulled into Red Deer in time for a late lunch. Red Deer bills itself as a "Nuclear Weapons Free Zone." This made us feel safer than we'd felt on the entire trip thus far.

Heading into downtown Red Deer is a fun experience, except for the gauntlet of traffic lights, which make the experience not really fun at all. I believe I read a stat once that suggested the average Red Deer resident spends something like eighteen years of their life stopped at Red Deer traffic lights. Anyone up for a Traffic Lights Free Zone?

In addition to lunch, we found the monument to one of Red Deer's most famous residents—Francis the Pig. The monument includes a statue of Francis, with a rock inscribed with the story of how Francis, in July 1990, escaped a local abattoir and somehow managed to elude predators and recapture attempts for five months. When finally captured, Francis the fugitive oinker was paroled to a local farm, where she lived a long and healthy life (presumably until someone got a hankering for a little bacon).

The monument was built as a tribute to the importance of hog production in the area, as opposed to celebrating the tenacity and willpower of a local resident destined for the breakfast plate.

In the annals of great pig escapes, Francis is truly another Alberta giant.

Francis, the most courageous pig in the west.

?

We bailed off of Highway 2 at Lacombe and headed east along Highways 50 and 53. Our next gigantic destination? Donalda, "Home of the World's Largest Lamp!" and the "Lamp Capital of Canada!"

The giant lamp is immediately obvious when you pull into Donalda. (That's one advantage of putting up giant things in small rural towns—you never have to ask for directions to them.)

Making like a pair of well-dressed moths, we walked right inside the Plexiglas 18-metre-high gas-burning lamp.

"Yup, it's big all right," I said to my wife.

"I bet people say that a lot," she replied, at which point we decided we would refrain from saying that for the rest of the Albertan Giants Road Tour.

The gas lamp looks a little like a gargantuan brown genie lantern. It is lit every night for the entire night, save for the time some kids climbed inside it in the middle of the night and shut the sucker down, causing a bit of concern in the otherwise peaceful little town of Donalda.

Across from the lamp sits the Donalda Museum, home of the world's largest collection of gas-burning lamps (more than 900). Inside, I flipped open the first scrapbook I saw, guessing it would contain interesting tidbits about the giant lamp or gas lamps in general. Instead I was surprised to find a whole raft of newspaper clippings, photos, and assorted memorabilia relating to one of Donalda's most famous residents—supermodel (whatever happened to just plain old models?) Tricia Helfer.

So now I was faced with an enormous dilemma: scan through the numerous photos of a gorgeous supermodel or look at gas lamps. Fortunately, my wife was along to help make the decision for me.

I never knew there were so many different kinds of lamps.

Farther east, we drove past Hughenden, home to two giants, a giant flower and, more curiously, a giant slingshot. The slingshot was missing its giant strap, so really it was just a giant slingshot handle. Nonetheless, it was still rather impressive.

I had seen a photo of the slingshot somewhere and a sign in the foreground that read "Canada Strikes Back," making me think someone must have built the slingshot as a helpful way to add to Canada's military might. Between the slingshot and the submarines at West Edmonton Mall, I knew our province was in safe hands. At least if Saskatchewan ever attacked.

At Chauvin, near the Saskatchewan border, we said a quick hello to Susie, "The World's Largest Softball," not to be confused with Dave, "The World's Largest Baseball," which, Lord knows, is probably out there somewhere. The 1.8-metre-diameter softball was built in 1977 to recognize the annual softball tournament in Chauvin. Her deliciously thick red lips and bright blue come-hither eyes somehow made her strangely erotic to me, which meant it was time to get out of Chauvin. Quickly.

Susie, the sexiest softball on the planet.

?

After a restful night's sleep dreaming of sexy softballs, we hit the road early and headed through the thick morning fog to Dewberry—"Home of the World's Largest Chuckwagon." I hate to say it, because I don't want to offend any more people than I already have, but this proved to be a bit of a disappointment.

I'm no expert on chuckwagons, but, to me, the world's largest chuckwagon looked smaller than many of the chuckwagons I've seen in my life, which is clearly not something you expect from the world's largest anything.

Now, I'm sure the fine residents of Dewberry have verified this, and perhaps it is larger by, say, one or two metres, but when a fellow goes out of his way to see the world's largest chuckwagon, a fellow really expects to see something, well, you know, how do I put this? Oh yeah, really, really big.

(After doing a bit of research, I did manage to find out that the Dewberry chuckwagon is fully functional, which made me feel better, and that it is one and a half times larger than a normal chuckwagon. So I apologize if I offended any giant chuckwagon aficionados. Even if the wagon isn't a hundred times the normal size, I must say that Dewberry is a quiet and pretty little corner of Alberta, and well worth a visit. So please don't write me any angry letters.)

The world's largest Easter egg, in Vegreville, would not, however disappoint. Vegreville has a rich Ukrainian heritage, hence the giant Easter egg, and not, say, a giant slab of back bacon.

The highway signs along the Yellowhead Highway advertise the attraction as the "World's Largest Pysanka," which made me wonder how many thousands of motorists drive by these signs each year and say "Huh?" After all, I'm sure many folks think a pysanka is a type of vegetable or a small rodent from Uruguay, so allow me to clear up any confusion. "Pysanka" is the Ukrainian term for Easter egg, derived from the Ukrainian verb *pysaty*, meaning "to write."

The pysanka sits in a pleasant park on the way into town, about 2 kilometres off Highway 16. It was unveiled in time to commemorate Queen Elizabeth II's visit in August 1978. I'm sure, at some point, some folks involved in the project probably thought "What's wrong with a nice box of bonbons?"

You see, not only is the egg large, it is an impressive feat of engineering. So much so that the design and construction required the help of eggheads from the University of Utah and, quite possibly, NASA. When all was said and done (which may or may not have included a little cussing at some point), nine engineering, architectural, and mathematical firsts were achieved, and it took more than 12,000 man-hours to complete. (And you thought painting Easter eggs with your four-year-old was a challenge.) One of the accomplishments is the first ever construction of an authentic egg shape, unless you count chickens. Presumably this is the first *human-made* construction of a genuine egg-shaped object.

The three colours used for the egg—silver, bronze, and gold—symbolize prosperity. In addition to welcoming the Queen, the egg symbolizes the harmony of early Ukrainian settlers in the area and celebrates the police force, which brought peace and order to the region. Again, wouldn't a nice thank-you card and box of chocolates have sufficed? One plaque also suggests the pysanka helps recognize "100 years of cultural progress in Alberta."

Cultural progress in Alberta? Ah yes, they must be talking about the giant sausage in Mundare. We were getting hungry, and a giant sausage seemed the perfect cure.

The world's largest pysanka prepares for takeoff.

for those of you into this sort of thing, here are the stats on vegreville's giant pysanka:

7.8 metres long, 5.5 metres wide, 9.5 metres tall.

The aluminum skin weighs 907 kilograms.

The internal structure weighs 1,360 kilograms.

The base supporting the egg weighs 12,247 kilograms.

The egg includes 524 star patterns, 2,208 triangular pieces, 3,512 visible facets, and 6,978 nuts and bolts (offering up an obvious diversion for the wee ones on your next trip to Vegreville).

Mundare, "The Small Town with the Big Heart," sits just a few minutes to the northwest of Vegreville.

"You'd have to have a big heart, what with all the sausage they probably eat here," I suggested to my wife.

The sausage sits alongside the main thoroughfare of Highway 855, just across from a gas station in a small park. Now, you're probably wondering, if you are at all normal, one simple thing: Why a giant sausage?

The reason is simply that this is sausage country. Mundare (population 5,000+) is home to the Stawnichy Meat Processing Plant, which produces some of the most famous sausage in the land of Alberta and is credited with bringing "the art of sausage making to a new level." A sign at the giant piece of meat explains that the structure celebrates a century of sausage-making in the area and suggests that Mundare is synonymous with "sausage."

According to the gas station attendants, many a visitor stops in to ask one simple question: "What the heck is that thing anyway?" Although you can clearly see it is indeed a giant sausage (or more correctly, a giant garlic ring), one might also mistake it for a giant intestine. Then it occurred to me that one might also mistake a real sausage for a piece of intestine, depending on how much champagne one had in one's orange juice, which further got me thinking, what *is* a sausage anyway?

The 14-metre-high sausage comes with a small viewing platform, in case you want to peer right up underneath the belly of the beast, making it the hands-down winner of the Oddest Viewing Platform Award in all of Alberta.

The giant sausage that ate Mundare.

I have to admit that as an enticing come-on, the sausage works. After twenty minutes or so of deep sausage staring and contemplation, we headed to a deli to sample the local meats, which was well worth the stop. Especially the sausage milkshake.

Dropping back down to Highway 16, we listened to a bit of talk radio to help bide the time. Who were these people phoning in the middle of the week with their solutions to all of life's woes?

One woman phoned in to tear a strip off a previous caller who'd degraded fruitcakes. Another caller from Edmonton let the world know he would root for the Russians over the Calgary Flames when it came to hockey. Still another had all the solutions to our economic woes.

"Don't these people have jobs?" I asked my wife.

"Why don't you phone in and ask?" she replied.

I almost did, until I realized she'd tricked me.

Driving the Yellowhead gives you a lot of time to think about the complexities of the world we live in. For example, just what does Carly Simon mean when she sings there are "clouds in my coffee" in the hit song "You're So Vain"? Was she mountain climbing or something?

Also, if we want teenagers to *not* watch some of the adult-oriented programming on television, why are we letting them know that "the following program contains scenes of nudity and sex"? Isn't this a surefire way of getting them to tune in every night? Wouldn't it be better to have a preprogram disclaimer such as "The following program contains mind-numbing scenes of boredom as we take a journey into the exciting world of fifteenth-century Russian linens"?

Then my brain switched gears, back to the story at hand. Why were Albertans obsessed with size? Why would people drive halfway across the province to visit a giant sausage? What's wrong with me, anyway?

As we passed Elk Island National Park, I was reminded of a funny story I heard back in my naturalist days. The story involves an Elk Island park naturalist talk starring "Annie the Aspen" and "Bruce the Spruce," who were on a journey to enlighten their audience about forest succession in Alberta—the story of how a forest begins and changes slowly over time, eventually maturing into a climax forest. On one particular evening, Bruce the Spruce missed his cue and trundled on stage a little early, prompting Annie the Aspen to loudly exclaim, "You're too early! I haven't reached climax yet!"

?

After staying overnight in Edmonton, we went in search of the world's largest badminton racquet, supposedly found in St. Albert, just north of Edmonton. I say "supposedly" because nobody I asked had heard of it.

"You sure you don't mean a giant sausage?" one girl asked me.

"Are you mistaking us for St. Paul?" another local asked.

"Are you thinking of a giant ping-pong racquet?" asked another.

"What the hell's your problem?" asked the last person I stopped for directions.

Finally someone knew what I meant and sent us off to the St. Albert racquet club centre. Expecting again to find a towering, looming racquet, one that King Kong himself might enjoy playing with, I was a tad disappointed to see merely a really, really big badminton racquet. It was nice and all, don't get me wrong. I'm just saying don't drive the in-laws up from Medicine Hat to see the world's biggest badminton racquet unless you also have plans for a nice lunch somewhere along the way.

One tends to think of rural Alberta as being the champions when it comes to giant stuff. However, Edmonton is no slouch in this area, being home to the world's largest mall, the world's largest hammer, the world's biggest shopping bag, the world's largest cowboy boot, a giant baseball bat, a giant beer can, and the world's largest milk bottle.

I was giddy with excitement as we pulled into Morinville, just north of St. Albert, so giddy that my wife told me to "giddy down"—you don't hear that every day, especially in cowboy country.

Edmonton is home to
more than just giant
shopping malls . . .

The reason for my excitement? Morinville is home to the world's largest toque. Here, at long last, was a giant attraction truly reflective of our Canadian heritage.

My elation quickly turned to heartache, however, upon learning that the toque was no more.

"What happened?" I asked, more than a little dumbfounded, a tear trickling down my left cheek.

"Mice," the town official replied.

"Excuse me?"

"Mice broke in and chewed up the toque. The little bastards."

After composing myself, all I could think to say was, "Well at least they weren't rats, which is some consolation, especially since we don't have any rats in Alberta."

Here's the lowdown on the former giant toque. It was 4.5 metres high, with a 12-metre circumference, more than enough to make it into the *Guinness Book of World Records*, and more than enough room for 106 kids to fit inside it, shattering the old record of 30 people inside a toque. Taking six weeks to make, it was stitched together by 113 volunteers ranging in age from eight to ninety-three. It even came with a giant pompom, making the heartbreak that much worse.

The loss of the toque truly is a shame, and I really do hope someone in Morinville rises to the challenge to create an even bigger toque, because if there's one thing Canada needs right now, it's a really, really big toque.

Making our way east again, we began knocking off giant things at a fast and furious rate.

First to Andrew, "Home of the World's Largest Mallard Duck" (7.6-metre wingspan, 2,268 kilograms), where a humongous duck statue pays homage to nearby Whitford Lake, a major waterfowl resting area.

Next up, Smoky Lake, the "Pumpkin Capital of Alberta" and home to a fairly big pumpkin, but somehow "fairly big pumpkin" doesn't quite generate the kind of excitement you want from your giant foodstuff.

As we approached Vilna, a sign advertising "Tourist Trap" made me smile. At last someone was practising a little truth in advertising. Vilna is, as everyone knows, "Home of the World's Largest Mushrooms." There were three 6-metre-high mushrooms sitting in the little park, replicas of the *Tricholoma uspale* variety, a traditional ingredient found in the region's ethnic dishes.

We ended our day at Lac La Biche, home of "The World's Smallest Airport" (for remote-controlled planes) and the V & H Drive-In burger joint, featuring the Mars or Bust Space Dock for travelling aliens and a sign proudly proclaiming "We will serve anybody from Planet Earth to Mars."

My kind of place.

?

The following morning, still heading east, we soon spotted our first directional sign leading us to "The World's Largest Pyrogy," in Glendon—"The Pyrogy Capital of Canada."

I stopped the car at one point to photograph the pyrogy

Finally, some truth in advertising.

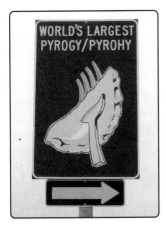

directional sign and wondered why it was that the cows always seemed to look at me like I'm an idiot for doing this.

"I don't think it's just the cows," my wife said.

The pyrogy capital, home to some five hundred pyrogy-loving Albertans, sits 1 kilometre south of Highway 660. The signs that promote the ever-nearing pyrogy, including the last one—"Pyrogy Straight Ahead!"—helped to create an aura of mouth-watering excitement as we drove into town.

The giant pyrogy sits in a park along Pyrogy Drive, right across from the Pyrogy Park Restaurant, quite possibly the only Chinese restaurant in the world that specializes in pyrogies.

The statue, which includes an equally impressive fork cutting through it, at first glance looks like a giant replica of Mr. Spock's Vulcan ear. On second glance, it looks like a giant replica of Mr. Spock's ear with a giant fork through it.

The enormous pyrogy was unveiled in 1991 by the Official Pyrogy Committee. (This makes sense, because let me tell you, if you are going to put up a giant pyrogy, the first thing you'll need is to get yourself a giant pyrogy committee. And make it an official one, so folks don't confuse it with any unofficial pyrogy committees, which tend to always add too much sour cream.)

There is a time capsule on site to be opened in 2016, containing, I would hope, a large vat of sour cream to go with the pyrogy.

Would you like fries with that?

The 9-metre-high, 2,722-kilogram fibreglass pyrogy was trucked in from BC, and it took four days and two cranes to put it together. Although it's not as complex as Vegreville's giant pysanka, I imagine that someone, somewhere, stared at a lot of pyrogies to get it just right.

Not everyone was excited to see the arrival of the gigantic pyrogy, however. As you may well imagine, these giant Albertan attractions attract their share of naysayers and controversy. A giant sausage, for example, did not necessarily send all hearts aflutter in Mundare, no matter how big their hearts may be. In Glendon, the idea of a huge pyrogy was by no means a slam dunk either.

In fact, a retired Glendon schoolteacher attempted to rally the anti-pyrogy forces in town. She surveyed 165 houses and found that only 24 percent approved of the pyrogy, while a whopping 41 percent called it "tacky, depressing and degrading to Ukrainians." An article in *Alberta Report*, if you'll pardon the pun, panned the pyrogy. Someone else I interviewed, who wished to remain anonymous, felt the pyrogy more closely resembles a part of the female anatomy. Yet another Glendonite summed up some of the local feelings at the time: "We should have put up a giant moose or something. Who is going to come here to look at a pyrogy?"

Well, as it turns out, a lot of folks. The giant pyrogy merited a mention in American humorist Dave Barry's weekly column, and the village office has received curious phone calls from as far away as Pennsylvania. There are pyrogy T-shirts, postcards, and coffee mugs for sale, an annual pyrogy festival during the September long weekend, and even a poem in honour of the stuffed dumpling. In 2002, Glendon held the first annual Pyrogy Bonspiel curling tournament, awarding trophies shaped like replicas of the giant pyrogy. A few local business merchants I talked to said that sales were definitely up due to the presence of the massive pyrogy, although they do get tired of people asking them what it's stuffed with. There is now even a guided tour that takes visitors via bus to all the giant things in the region, with Glendon's pyrogy being a star attraction along the route.

"So, what do you think, honey?" I asked my wife as we sat at the park, studying the pyrogy.

"I think all these giant food things are going to make us fat," she replied.

"You're right," I said. "I could definitely go for a pyrogy."

Our final stop on our Albertan Giants Road Tour was, appropriately enough, at St. Paul, Alberta, whose town slogan, "Out of this World," celebrates its UFO landing pad.

Now this isn't necessarily in keeping with the road trip's theme. After all, I'm sure there are larger UFO landing sites (such as the State of Florida). But St. Paul *did* have the foresight to build the world's *first* official UFO landing pad.

The UFO landing pad and flying saucer visitor centre are located along the main street of St. Paul, on Galaxy Way, next to an auto parts shop (which is good, as aliens will likely need to stock up on a few parts for the old spaceship) and a school (again convenient, as the aliens will need plenty of small children to fuel the next leg of their journey).

St. Paul's UFO landing pad awaits E.T.'s imminent arrival.

A sign at the bottom of the stairway leading to the pad greets intergalactic travellers with the following message:

> Republic of St. Paul
> (Stargate Alpha)
> The area under the world's first UFO landing pad was designated international by the town of St. Paul as a symbol that mankind will maintain the outer universe free from national wars and strife. That future travel in space will be safe for all intergalactic beings. All visitors from Earth or otherwise are welcome to this territory and to the town of St. Paul.

It's a nice sentiment. Of course, I wasn't sure that my own neighbourhood could even maintain a strife-free existence, so it seemed a rather lofty goal.

A message on a second plaque waxes even more eloquently, reminding us not to forget our failures on planet Earth, urging us to learn the true meaning of tolerance. The declaration ends like this: "If we cannot develop international goodwill among all men, how shall we ever develop intergalactic goodwill among other beings. Lastly, if mankind travels this earth or universe armed with kindness, tolerance, hope, and good spirits, he will always be welcomed."

"Wow," I said to my wife. "Hard to argue with that."

"Why are they just talking about mankind? Why didn't they mention women? If they want to extend goodwill to Saturn, shouldn't they start with me?"

"Of course, my petite pamplemousse," I said, "but you see, this sign, this entire monument, was built in 1967, back when—"

"When men were more interested in purple aliens with nine ears than the fairer sex, I understand. That's why women are slowly taking over the world. You don't even know it's happening, do you?"

"Do I what?"

"Exactly."

We strolled up the cement staircase to the pad itself. The Canadian flag, along with all the provincial and territorial flags, stands at attention at the back of the 12-metre platform. The pad is round, because, as far as we knew in 1967, all spaceships were round. It's not a huge parking space, offering parking for one economy-sized landing craft.

"They should install a parking meter here, you know, earn a little revenue off them when they land," I suggested to the information attendant inside the flying saucer–shaped information centre.

She explained the story of the landing pad. Turns out it was a centennial project in honour of Canada's birthday. The Feds responded to a proposal by the town to build the landing pad with a generous donation. In fact this and other projects helped St. Paul nab the honour of being Canada's Centennial Town.

"I think they thought St. Paul was the perfect place to build it because there are so many aliens already here walking amongst us," she said. "It's only a matter of time that the mother ship will return for them."

This made my wife and I back slowly away from the counter. That and the fact that a third arm had just appeared from behind the attendant's back.

The information centre also doubles as a UFO centre for Alberta, with UFO exhibits downstairs, a UFO hotline, and a small gift shop selling UFO-related things, such as T-shirts reading "My parents were abducted by aliens and all I got was this lousy T-shirt."

On the drive home, my wife sound asleep and snoring like a Klingon, I mentally retraced our road trip, checking off all the strange things we had seen. If aliens were to land among us at St. Paul one day, what would they think of our goofy attractions? Or worse, if they arrive a millennium from now, and there's nothing left of us (because at the rate our stupidity seems to be growing, I have serious doubts we'll still be here) except for these giant things, what story about us will they piece together?

Surely, any reasonably with-it alien would have to believe we were a primitive species who lived among different clans and worshipped some very strange gods. Our symbols honouring the God of Meat and the God of Boiled Dumplings will let them know that we were a species who cared a great deal about food. The giant pysanka will likely be explained away as a mock spaceship. And the remains of the giant T. Rex will be slowly pieced together to reveal the horrifying creature that, in the end, must have killed us off.

As I turned south onto Highway 2 and merged with the other humanoids, I wondered if I had learned anything at all about Alberta's obsession with size. There was certainly no sign that the big-things-mania craze was slowing. Beaverlodge was about to erect a giant beaver, while Whitecourt was plotting to build the world's biggest snowmobile.

Was it all being done *just* to lure unsuspecting tourists off the main highways? Had we taken the rallying cry from the film *Field of Dreams*—"If you build it, they will come"—just a wee bit too far? Surely there is more to it than that?

Is it because we have so much space in Alberta that we feel a need to stretch skyward? Or are we trying to leave our mark on the planet so future generations know and understand that these small communities were here and that they mattered? In this day and age of falling grain elevators and dying rural towns, I'd like to think it's a bit of the latter.

I pulled onto the Trans-Canada Highway, road weary and glad to be finally near home again. Then I came upon a truck whose bumper sticker summed up the entire trip rather nicely: "Go BIG or Go HOME!"

things you really ought to know about alberta

The Central Alberta Sasquatch Research Web site lists 124 sasquatch sightings reported from Alberta.

Wetaskiwin passed a law in 1917 stating "A male and female horse must not be tied together on Main Street."

The Seebe, Alberta, curling rink (recently closed), featuring only a single sheet of ice, is listed in the *Guinness Book of World Records* as the world's smallest curling rink.

Alberta legislation allows $25 fines for anyone refusing to change his or her clock to daylight savings time. So far, no one has been charged with this heinous offence.

alberta: the rat-free province

Alberta is proudly 100 percent rat-free. That's right—we have *no* rats. It's actually guaranteed in our constitution. Our rat-free status is a source of pride second only to our absence of any provincial sales tax. In fact, here's a conversation I overheard recently on a flight to Toronto:

> Non-Albertan: "So, where are you from?"
>
> Albertan: "Alberta. We don't have any provincial sales tax."
>
> Non-Albertan: "I know, I know."
>
> Albertan: "But did you also know that we don't have any rats either? None. Zippo. Nada. So, where are you from?"
>
> Non-Albertan: "Toronto."
>
> Albertan (after the laughter subsides): "Toronto? Oh my god, you're crawling in rats! You've got more rats than people, don't you? You know, we have no rats in Alberta."
>
> Non-Albertan: "What do you mean 'no rats'? That's impossible."
>
> Albertan: "No, no it's not. We have none. It's in our constitution."
>
> Non-Albertan: "You have a constitution?"
>
> Albertan: "Of course, it's Alberta. We have everything! Except a provincial sales tax. And rats."

Of course, not all conversations go like this. Sometimes the other person is from Newfoundland.

But just imagine this for a moment: No sales tax. And no rats. And even if we had rats, *we wouldn't have to pay any provincial sales tax to purchase one.* Is your head reeling? I mean, is Alberta paradise or what? I bet you're thinking "Is this some sort of utopian dreamland?" No, no it's not. It's just little old Alberta. PST-free, debt-free, rat-free—and proud of it.

Short of sending Members of Parliament off to Ottawa, how does a province obtain rat-free status? I'm glad you asked, because I did some investigative journalism to look into the matter, because that's what investigative journalists do. Here's what I found out.

We do have bushy-tailed *wood rats* in Alberta, found in the Canadian Rockies, which are prone to stealing hubcaps and dishwashers, but these aren't the rats that concern us here. We're talking about *real* rats, the ratty kind of rats: Norway rats that sneak in under the radar and chew insulation, destroy agricultural food crops, undermine buildings with their tunnelling activities, and spread nasty diseases. (I had neighbours exactly like this once, and I can attest that you don't want to have anything to do with them.)

So why are we rat-free? Well, according to a Government of Alberta Web site, they don't enter the province from the south because of the sparse southern population. (Rats enjoy hanging with people and can't overwinter in sparsely populated areas.) And, although this isn't mentioned per se on the Web site, I feel it's also because of the tight anti-terrorist restrictions now in place along the U.S. border. The little darlings don't come in from the west either because our mountains prove to be a formidable barrier to rats, not to mention a few British Columbians. And from the north we're covered because of the sparse population and boreal forests.

Which just, once again, leaves the east as our only serious problem (like *that's* a big surprise)—our weakest link, our Achilles heel. The Saskatchewan-Alberta border is North America's longest unprotected *straight* surveyed line. Like Feds drawn to burgeoning oil revenues, rats can smell this from miles away. This is the front line for Alberta's ongoing WAR ON RATS. (It's much more dramatic if you capitalize it, don't you think?)

Although many rats, anxious to see the new world, came to Canada in 1775, and although rats entered Saskatchewan in the 1920s, we've managed to keep the rats at bay or, at least, in Saskatchewan. In fact, here's an amazing example of just how far-sighted, for once, our government was when it came to rats: the government had legislation already in place authorizing an anti-rat program *even before we had rats.* (If only it had the same foresight when it came to health care and education, but I digress.)

Thus, when the first of the little buggers made forays into our province (much as certain people from Lloydminster are prone to doing) in the early 1950s, Alberta was prepared to initiate its anti-rat program the moment they crossed the line, before, as the government literature states, "anyone had a chance to get accustomed to them." This is good, because as soon as people get accustomed to rats, the next thing you know they'll be turning them into pets or inviting them over to watch the game. Then where would we be?

Still, to this day, we must be vigilant. The Department of Agriculture assumes responsibility for the rat control program, monitoring a 15,000-square-kilometre strip along the province's eastern border. Of course, it can't do it alone, which is where you folks come in. (I know, I know, it sort of worries me too.)

The first thing you need to know is that it is illegal to own a rat in Alberta, or to bring one into Alberta, for that matter. Which raises two questions: Why would anyone want to own a rat? Secondly, what's wrong with you people, anyway?

The second thing is that we need to have a lot of eyes and ears along the eastern front looking out for the furry little darlings. The problem here is that a lot of folks have trouble identifying rats, because, well, we don't have any (please see above). So the anti-rat squad (as only I am allowed to call them) receives many false alarms from people mistaking gophers, mice, bushy-tailed wood rats, chihuahuas, coyotes, men with really, really bad toupees, and, oddly enough, the occasional wayward moose with the dreaded Norway rats.

In the interest of learning more about Norway rats, I took a couple of fun rat quizzes on the Alberta Agriculture Web site and am pleased to report that I scored very well on both. In fact, I'm seriously thinking of entering the International Rat Trivia Olympics, being held in Helsinki in 2012. I'm also pleased to say that the quiz contains some delightful humour, such as in question 12:

Rats that live in man-made structures are called:

a. lazy

b. squatters

c. commensal

(Curiously, I've used all three terms to describe some of my relatives at one point or another.)

Other questions ask if rats travelled throughout the world via alien ships (which I believe is true) and if the most notice-able thing about a Norway rat is its laugh (not well known, but also true, especially once they've got into your still).

Do yourself, and more importantly your fellow Albertans, a favour and become more rat-aware. You wouldn't want us to lose our much-coveted rat-free status, would you? It's in our constitution, after all.

A tourist complains to a park warden about safety along the Icefields Parkway, the mountain highway between Lake Louise and Jasper.

"That road is so windy, with all those cliffs you really should put up more guardrails," the man says.

"We can't," the warden replies. "It's too expensive to replace them because the tourists keep knocking them down."

———————————

"Do people fall off Mt. Rundle very often?" a tourist asks a park warden.

"No. Just once," the warden replies.

questions asked by visitors to the rockies

At what elevation does an elk become a moose?

How do the elk know to cross at the elk crossing signs?

Are the hot springs hot?

Can you go into the hot springs in the rain, or will you get wet?

Have the mountains moved since the last time we were here?

Are the national parks natural or manmade?

Do you need tampons to hike over the glaciers?

How many undiscovered lakes are there in the Rockies?

If I'm camping in Banff, should I leave my bacon out on the picnic table or bring it into the tent with me?

Is it true that to escape a bear, you have to climb a tree that's the same width as your head?

things you need to know about banff national park

It's a national park.

B anff is a national park, which means it is run by the Feds, but please don't hold that against the place—it truly is a spectacular chunk of the planet, and a wonderful place to pick up an extra T-shirt.

National parks are set aside to protect natural and cultural heritage for *all* Canadians. This means that, unlike in Alberta's provincial parks, you may encounter some non-Albertans. Please be polite to them at all times, and try not to feed them no matter how persistent they may be.

Expect to see more than just a few folks when you visit. Banff receives close to five million visitors annually, all in pursuit of the same goal: to get away from it all. Ironic, isn't it?

It's in Canada, eh.

Not only is Banff a national park, it's now (according to the entrance sign along the Trans-Canada Highway) Banff National Park *of Canada*. The change coincided with all those flag-plastering, flag-waving, ad-scam scandals in Quebec, but I'm sure it's just a freak coincidence that in no way relates to this story, even though some Parks Canada folks were quoted at the time as saying that the changes had "something vaguely to do with Quebec and separation and reminding Quebecers that national parks are national and blah blah blah . . . " But I'm still certain it's all just a happy coincidence.

Evidently, all national parks now go by the "of Canada" qualifier. In addition to the reasons noted above, the government just likes to make things as long as possible. Having worked for the federal government, I can honestly say that one of its mottoes is "Never use 10 words when 185 will do the trick."

As well as complying with this federally regulated guideline pressing for maximum verbosity, "of Canada" lets wayward visitors know that they have not inadvertently entered Banff National Park of Lithuania, which is a common mistake many travellers make, especially folks from Ontario.

Finally, adding "of Canada" resulted in the creation of several thousand jobs for sign manufacturers. Unbeknownst to most Canadians, roughly 87 percent of federal government expenditures goes toward the manufacturing of new signs, vehicle identifiers, and assorted labels. This age-old job creation technique has been employed by successive governments for as long as government has existed. This is why, you may have noticed, government agencies love nothing better than to change their names every three months, then change them back to whatever they were before, every nine months.

But I digress. The point is, please always refer to our national park treasures, such as Banff and Jasper, by their proper, full names, even in casual conversation. On behalf of sign painters and great Canadians everywhere, I thank you for your ongoing support of this great nation.

All national park visitors require a valid park permit.

The park pass is sort of like the entrance pass you get to go into Disneyland, only, unlike Disneyland, you'll have to pay extra to go on all the rides. Also unlike Disneyland, the large furry animals wandering around are liable to attack you. Otherwise, it's a very similar experience.

The higher you get, the higher you get.

This is an old climber's saying, said, especially by old climbers, to describe what happens when you move higher in elevation. What happens, of course, is there is less oxygen as you gain elevation, which means people, not unlike yourself, are prone to being a little oxygen-deprived when visiting the Rockies. This can cause people, not unlike yourself, to say and do really stupid things, because, as we all know, the brain needs lots of oxygen in order to photosynthesize properly.

In fact, researchers into the effects of high altitude warn

that a lack of oxygen can impair cerebral functions, including the ability to perform tasks quickly, remember, and discriminate. (This explains so much about the years I lived in Lake Louise, Canada's highest community.)

So unless you are a Tibetan Sherpa or have nested all your life in Denver, be prepared for a little more heavy breathing than you may be comfortable with around complete strangers.

It is illegal to feed the animals.

Hand feeding the animals takes on whole new meaning when you realize you no longer have a hand from which to feed the adorable animals because some little bugger has just ripped it off your wrist and is now playing with it like it's a dead rat.

So please don't hand feed them, don't leg feed them, don't bag feed them, and don't throw any food their way. If you do, you are—in a word—really, really stupid. All right, that's three words, but you deserve three words. (And why use only one word when you can use three?)

The electric "bear fence" surrounding the Lake Louise of Canada campground is designed to keep *you in*, not the bears out.

Ditto for the wildlife fence along the Trans-Canada Highway. This is in recognition that it is you, the park visitor, who is the most dangerous animal in the Rockies and that you must be contained at all costs before anyone gets seriously hurt.

The park wardens are still not armed.

And I do mean with guns, because most of them, thankfully, come with arms included. Although "Sheila's Cops" fought valiantly for the right to be armed and dangerous, they lost the battle and now must contend with just being dangerous.

So, as it has always been, if a park warden encounters a rifle-toting poacher in the park's far back country or a nefarious criminal in a routine campground patrol, their only line of defense is some really, really harsh words accompanied by a very mean look.

Not to worry—all wardens must go through intensive training on how to look really, really mean. Park wardens stress that they don't like to use this mean look and will do so only as an absolute last resort, and only when they have exhausted all other possible means for a safe and peaceful resolution.

Don't stop at the bear jams and gawk.
I mean *really*, do bears come by your house and watch you? I didn't think so.

Play safe or go home.
If you're going out into the mountains, please reconsider immediately. Then, if you are still gung-ho on risking the lives of everyone around you, please play safe by taking a few extra precautions. (Like reconsidering once again and staying home.)

First, let people know where you are going. It doesn't matter who these people are, just tell someone, even if they don't care the slightest whit about you.

Second, stay on the trails and don't take any shortcuts. Shortcuts may initially appear to be a faster way down the mountain, but that's because everything seems faster when you're freefalling for three thousand metres.

Third, stay away from other visitors. According to statistics, you are thirty-four times more likely to be killed by a human than by an animal.

Finally, don't be a goofball. Being a goofball might be an okay way to make a life for yourself in the city, but in the mountains, it can pose a serious problem. So don't place your child on the back of a moose, don't bungee jump off the Johnson Canyon catwalk, don't try to snowboard on the Columbia Icefield, and for goodness sake, don't run naked through the alpine meadows, because *no one* wants to see that.

The hot springs are not clothing-optional.
I mention this because, sadly, on a few occasions, visitors to the hot pools have gotten so absorbed in thought, they have forgotten to put on their bathing suits before entering the pools. Please don't make that mistake.

Watch where you stop for a pee.
I mention *this*, not because I was thinking about people peeing in the hot springs, but because I once witnessed a bear jam along the Icefields Parkway that was caused not by a bear, but by some poor fellow who had pulled over to have a quick pee.

On a related cautionary note, there is the oft-told story of a local Banffite who, presumably in an effort to ward off wild animals, peed around the perimeter of his tent, only to awaken the following morning to the sound of an elk peeing on his tent.

Sadly, it doesn't stop there. There is also the tale of a man who emerged from his tent for a pee one moonless night and ended up peeing on a black bear, causing the offended bruin to swat the man's bare behind.

So, to recap: watch where you pee.

If you want to move to Banff, you must pass the stringent "need to reside" rule.

I include this advice because once you've visited Banff, you'll be bit by the I-want-to-live-in-Banff-and-wake-up-to-the-sounds-of-chirping-birds-and-humping-elk-for-the-rest-of-my-life bug.

To limit the growth of the town of Banff and provide adequate staff housing, *only* people who have a *legitimate* need to live there for *legitimate* work purposes are allowed to take up residence. This strict—some might argue draconian—need to reside clause ensures that the *only* people allowed to live within the town limits are Parks Canada employees; tourist business operators and staff; essential service providers; retired athletes, coaches, and astronauts; former or current politicians; banjo salesmen; former Miss America beauty queens; licensed bagpipe tuners; marine biologists; aestheticians; people who have appeared on the game show *Jeopardy*; left-handed people; anyone with the middle name Norman (or who knows of someone named Norman); people who have an extensive knowledge of termites or of Bulgaria; or anyone who has a relative, friend, or business associate who can vouch for their existence.

You're probably thinking, "Wow. I don't have a hope in hell of ever living in Banff." Don't be discouraged—if you feel you fall into one of the aforementioned categories, thereby qualifying as a potential candidate for residency, you must simply say to someone close to you, such as your spouse, "I have a deep-burning need to reside in Banff." (So, really, the process is not nearly as daunting as some people may have led you to believe.)

A hiker comes face to face with a grizzly bear on a trail in Banff National Park.

The hiker abruptly falls to his knees, raises his hands below his chin, and prays to God, "Please, Lord, please let this be a good Christian bear."

The man opens his eyes and watches in stunned amazement as the grizzly drops to its knees and begins to pray, "Lord, thank you for this meal I am about to receive."

————————

How do you stop a grizzly in Jasper from charging?

The same as anywhere else—take away its credit card.

————————

A tourist is chatting with a park warden in Waterton Lakes National Park.

"Is it true that I'll be safe from a grizzly attack if I carry a torch?" the man asks the warden.

The warden answers, "Depends how fast you can run with a torch."

warning: bear country ahead

Visitors to our glorious mountain national and provincial parks aren't being told the whole story when it comes to travelling in bear country. Sure, there are those handy warning signs with pithy suggestions such as "Bears are dangerous. Don't stick your head inside their jaws." And there are the brochures, such as the classic "You Are in Bear Country," which details some things you really do need to know, like never play hide n' seek with grizzly cubs. But, in my humble estimation, the signs and brochures simply don't go far enough.

Sadly, it is up to me to enlighten you—the uninformed and misguided masses—on some basic safety rules when travelling through bear country.

Survival of the loudest is the law of the land.
Make noise. Yes, make like a Jehovah's Witness and warn bears that you are entering their home, just as you would when you arrive on anyone's doorstep.

Although a lot of mountain gift shops sell bear bells, I do not recommend these. It is very difficult, not to mention dangerous, to get a bear to sit still long enough to put the bells on it.

Nor should you put the bear bells on you, for a few reasons. First, unless you're willing to haul around something the size of the Liberty Bell, these Tinkerbell-sized bear bells just aren't loud enough, and the whole idea is to warn a bear well in advance of your presence, not after tripping over its snout.

Second, hiking with these annoying little jingling bells will make you feel as though you're hiking with some Shriners or a pack of Santa's elves. Really, who wants that?

Finally, I don't know about you, but to me, a little tinkling bell means one thing and one thing only: dinner is served!

No, the best noise-maker is your voice, which, as an added bonus, adds no extra weight to your hiking pack. So just sing a song, yell like a banshee, or better yet, do what I do: use a pig call. A loud "soooooooo-eeeee" travels far and wide and is guaranteed to warn away any bear in the vicinity. (The downside is you may end up attracting pigs, so you'll have to make a judgment call here.)

If you run, they will catch you.

The oldest Alberta joke is probably this one:

"What's the number one rule when hiking in bear country?"

"Always bring along someone you can outrun."

This probably would work as a bear encounter strategy, especially if you trip your hiking partner, having previously stuffed a few pork chops down their pants or smeared honey inside their underwear. The problem with running away from a bear, however, is this: bears are damn fast. They can outdistance a racehorse in a short sprint. (Isn't that an event we'd all pay good money to see at Spruce Meadows sometime?)

Moreover, if you've been told to run downhill to escape a grizzly, because somehow grizzlies can't run downhill without collapsing into a series of Jerry Lewis–style pratfalls, this is just, well . . . really, really silly. Because with the help of a little thing called gravity and downhill momentum, grizzlies go even *faster* running downhill.

To recap: if you run, they will catch you.

They *are* likely to chase after you if you run because running will make you look like you've done something wrong, as though you're positively guilty of *something*. Have you ever met up with a police officer downtown and then turned and run really fast in the opposite direction? Trust me, they always chase after you. *Every* time.

Same thing with a bear. If you run, chances are that will excite its predatory instinct, which whispers, "Hmm. Why is that idiot running away from me? Could it be he's done something to piss me off? Or could it be that those generous buttocks might taste better than they actually look?" Then it's off to the races.

So, please, never run from a bear. (Or a police officer—unless you really have done something wrong.)

Everywhere is bear country.

Visitors to Alberta's mountain playground get a little confused by this notion of "bear country." Hence such questions as:

"How do I get to bear country?"

"Will I need my passport to get into bear country?"

"Did I miss bear country? Can you show me on the map where it's closest to?"

These people, often known as people-who-take-things-just-a-tad-too-literally-kind-of-people, are sadly confused and should probably be sent home immediately for their own safety and the safety of those around them.

You see, in the mountains, everywhere is bear country. Bear country really isn't so much a place, as a state of mind. Just consider the following examples.

An innovative bear once broke into the ice cream shop at the Chateau Lake Louise and gorged himself on ice cream. Another bruin discovered the automatic doors at Lake Louise's Post Hotel and began to stroll in—presumably looking for a warm, secure den site for the winter. One enterprising bear stole some meat off a barbecue from a third-storey balcony in a Banff apartment building. Another broke into a motorhome and stole a loaf of bread. And as detailed in the highly inform-ative and thought-provoking book *When Do You Let the Animals Out?*, a curious bear once made his way into some-one's parked car and nearly drove off with their vehicle along the Icefields Parkway.

I'm quite certain any folks involved in these incidents thought, at the time, they were clearly *not* in bear country. How foolish of them to think so.

Remember, *everywhere* is bear country, so the next time you are staying in a mountain hotel such as the Banff Springs Hotel, and you need to get up to pee at 3:00 AM, take your bear spray and make some noise. Because you just never know.

Pepper, anyone?

Bear pepper spray, similar to the pepper spray former prime minister Jean Chrétien joked about using with his meals and on APEC protesters, is now commonly recommended for folks travelling deep into bear country. (See above for details on how to find bear country.) It is available in two convenient sizes: small for small bears or big for big bears. I recommend the big size.

You can also purchase a holster for your bear spray. This allows you to roam the Rockies looking very much like a cowboy from the old west, only instead of a six-shooter, you're armed with a nice condiment. (Of course, you can also use the holster to carry along a can of air freshener, jar of mustard, or bottle of beer.)

The holster is a great idea—I have encountered far too many backpackers who've packed the spray at the bottom of their pack under eighty-seven pounds of crap. Unfortunately, most bears are not prone to waiting for you to fish through your eighty-seven pounds of crap. Using a holster allows quick access to the spray, while making a striking fashion statement at the same time.

Here's the important thing you need to know: read the directions. If you do, you'll discover that bear spray is meant to be sprayed as a last resort *onto* the bear, and that it is *not*, as some folks in Banff unfortunately discovered, to be used in a similar fashion as mosquito repellent. This is not some "Anti-Bear Repellent" that Batman would stash in his utility belt. No, the simple idea is to spray it in the bear's direction. And preferably not into a headwind.

Bear spray *is* classified as a weapon—a grandmother was jailed in southern Alberta for trying to carry it across the U.S. border. So please do not attempt to take it with you when crossing the border or going onto a plane (unless you feel there may be bears aboard your flight, in which case I would find a way to sneak it aboard).

Pick your spots.

There's a catchy saying to differentiate what one should do in a black bear encounter vs. a grizzly bear meeting, which goes like so: "If it's brown, lie down. If it's black, fight back."

The rule suggests that, as a last resort, if you are being threatened by a bear, you should fight back with a rock, stick, or your foot (better still, your friend's foot) if it's a black bear. But with a grizzly, your best bet is to make like a quivering lump of frightened flesh, because your odds of winning a fight against a grizzly are about the same as your spouse inviting Michael Jackson to your kid's next birthday party.

One problem with this saying is that sometimes black bears are brown, and sometimes grizzlies are black. You need to look beyond colour and watch for things like the hump on a grizzly's shoulder or the shape of its face to make sure you know who you're messing with.

Of course, playing dead is really very much a last resort. Don't play dead, for example, if you've spied a bear through your spotting scope on the other side of the valley or if you see one on the side of the road while driving at high speeds.

Also remember that 99.9 percent of the time, a grizzly is more frightened of you than you are of it. It'll be long gone before you ever have a chance to demonstrate your fine acting skills. (Ironic, isn't it? If only they knew how easily you'd crumble like a house of cards in quicksand.)

But let's suppose for a moment that you are unfortunate enough to be part of the 0.1 percent of folks whose bear refuses to be intimidated by the likes of you. What to do? Well, we've already ruled out running away screaming like a little girl. The first thing to do is stand perfectly still; make like a trembling aspen and send out some Zen-like vibes that you are not a threat. Grizzlies are primarily vegetarians, so they are most likely not thinking about smothering you in steak sauce. No, they're just concerned you're going to be a pain in the ass. They want some reassurance you aren't going to do something really stupid, because history has shown them time and time again that you are prone to doing stupid things.

So now is not the time or place to shout obscenities, throw rocks, or stare longingly into the grizzly's deep brown eyes. No, now is the time to chill. Look at the ground and perhaps say a few kind things to the bear in a low, calming tone, such as:

"Hey. My name's Joe. What's yours? Come here often?"

"That's a great hump you have. I bet the chicks really dig you."

"What's that smell? Is that you or me?"

If the bear is still not convinced and takes a run at you, don't be alarmed. Often these are only "bluff charges," much like calls from telemarketers.

If, however, it seems that your grizzly is intent on making an issue out of the whole encounter, you may want to play dead by dropping to the ground like a sack of soggy potatoes. And here, at long last, is where I come to my point—pick your spot.

A few years ago, some folks near the Canmore Nordic Centre, you see, chose to play dead underneath the very tree where mama bear had sent her cub. Not the best spot to play dead. On a similar note, a hunter from BC once climbed a tree to get away from a bear only to discover he had scaled the same tree her two cubs were hiding out in. (How do you know you are having a *really, really* bad day?)

So, when presented with a charging bear, take the time to look around a bit. While you're at it, you may as well choose a soft piece of land to play dead on—there's no sense in being uncomfortable for the whole experience. If all goes according to plan, the bear will merely sniff around a bit, rifle through your pockets for loose change, then be on her merry way, having determined that something this pathetic can't possibly pose a threat to anything other than itself.

I hope this information helps, because I enjoy being helpful. Incidentally, many of the techniques described above also work with teenagers, angry spouses, and telemarketers.

My brother-in-law from Saskatchewan isn't very bright—he still thinks Medicine Hat is a cure for head lice.

———————————

How dry is it in southern Alberta?

It's so dry … the trees go looking for dogs.

———————————

You can always tell people from southern Alberta: When the wind stops blowing, they topple over.

———————————

Two out of three people who move to Lethbridge stay there. The third gets blown to Medicine Hat.

After a terrible windstorm in southern Alberta, a rancher happens upon a cowboy hat lying on the ground. He picks it up and is shocked to find the head of his neighbour underneath it, buried up to his neck in sand.

"Holy smokes!" yells the rancher. "I'll go grab a shovel to dig you out of there!"

"You better get a tractor," the buried neighbour replies. "I'm sitting on a horse!"

Why is it so windy in southern Alberta?

Because BC blows and Saskatchewan sucks.

After a farmer from southern Alberta won eight million dollars in the lottery, a reporter asked him, "What do you plan to do with all the money you've won?"

The farmer thought for a moment, then replied, "Well, I guess I'll just keep farming until the money runs out."

the trip south

There's nothing like a great Canadian road trip. And this was *nothing* like a great Canadian road trip. You see, we weren't headed across Canada. No, we were headed south. South into the heartland of the hinterland of the wheat lands and Badlands and flatlands known as southern Alberta.

Yes, *this* was an *Alberta* road trip.

As I explained to my lovely and charming travelling companion (also known as my wife), the more one travels around Alberta, the more one feels like a true-blue Albertan. Or at least this was the theory we were about to test drive.

"But wouldn't Italy have been a nicer way to spend a romantic summer vacation?" my wife asked.

Wives. They can be so silly sometimes. And so unaffordable.

Day 1
Our first stop on our mini-epic occurred thirty-seven seconds into the trip. It was, naturally, for coffee. Like most Canadians, I am incapable of driving more than six blocks without a cup of java perched between my thighs. So two muffins, four doughnuts, twenty-four doughnut holes, and two very sticky thighs later, we were ready to hit the open road. Well, not so much the open road as much as the Trans-Canada Highway.

It was 30 June—the day before Canada Day—so fortunately there were only about 137,000 cars on the highway between Canmore and Calgary. All headed in the same direction we were. And all going at different speeds. What fun!

"Where are all these idiots headed?" I asked my wife.

"I don't know, where are *we* headed?" she replied.

Wives. So much fun to have along on road trips.

Twenty-five minutes into our trip, we ran into our first cows. Not literally, of course. That would be a bad thing, especially in Alberta, where cows are revered almost as much as they are in India (the only subtle difference being that we eat ours).

"There are more cows than people in Alberta," I told my wife, then warned her that we should expect to see more cows during our Alberta travels. Had she been awake to hear this comment, I'm sure she would have been as fascinated as you are right now.

While we're on the Trans-Canada Highway, literally, let's clear something up. The something up being this: "Trans-Canada" is a bit misleading. The name implies that you can actually cross Canada on this highway. Sure, technically, you *can* cross Canada on this massive artery. I've done it. But it takes four weeks. Three weeks to cross six provinces and one week to cross the giant hemorrhaging clot known as the city of Calgary. A directionally challenged, bull-legged gopher can cross Calgary faster than the average Trans-Canada–bound motorist.

Crossing Calgary, you see, requires stopping at approximately 312 traffic lights, none of which are synched with each other. Then there are the detours. And the pedestrians. The cyclists. The semis. The construction workers. The section of road that passes through a Plus 15 walkway. The portion that snakes through Peter's Drive-In drive-through lane. The portage across the Bow River. By day three, it can all get a little exhausting.

Fortunately, since we were heading south, we didn't have to worry about making that arduous east-west journey across Calgary. After a quick visit with my publisher to verify the massive travel budget for the trip ahead (gee, she sure is nice, and smells great, too), we were off through the bowels of southern Calgary, some of the largest bowels you'll find anywhere in Canada.

"My gosh, Calgary is a big city." This was my wife.

"Uh huh." This was me. There's nothing like the open road to stimulate interesting conversation.

She was right, though. Calgary is big, and getting more

massive by the second. This shocks many American visitors who, upon arrival, expect to find only a smattering of igloos and curling rinks or, at the very least, a small, rustic village nestled within a sea of untamed wilderness (much like visitors from Toronto expect). Alas, Calgary is the fifth most populous city in Canada. In terms of overall girth, it's a monster. Although not as bloated as Edmonton, it's still an impressive 722 square kilometres, which makes it larger than Waterton Lakes National Park. (I find it a rather disquieting notion to imagine that you can fit Waterton Lakes National Park inside Calgary and still have room for tens of thousands of urban dwellers and a couple of grizzly bears.)

But soon enough the Calgary city skyline was fading in our rearview mirror as we made our way south along Highway 2, the main artery connecting Lethbridge and Calgary.

We didn't head south for long, however. No, this was going to be a *fun* road trip—which meant plenty of side trips. So we veered off the freeway and headed for the sleepy little town of Okotoks. Surprisingly, my wife didn't know that Okotoks was a Native term meaning "Wow, is this a fun place or WHAT!" Okay, so that's not what Okotoks means. It actually means "Place where Tim Hortons offers more coffee for long road trip ahead." And, okay, so it's not a sleepy little town. Okotoks has become one of those booming Calgary bedroom communities, complete with beds, bedside tables, and nightlights.

We pulled into the first Tim Hortons we spied and asked the gal (that's Albertan talk for "girl") at the drive-through window where the big rocks were.

"The what?" she replied.

"The big rocks. You know, the famous Okotoks rocks. The rocks Okotoks is named for," I said. "*Surely*, you know about the rocks? The erratics?"

"Aren't the Erratics a rock band?" she asked.

"Well, maybe. But the erratics I'm thinking of are glacial erratics—large boulders left behind by a glacier during the last ice age."

"Oh. You mean the rocks," she said flatly, with about as much enthusiasm as one might muster for a self-administered frontal lobotomy. Evidently Okotokians aren't as excited about their rocks as their visitors are.

"I think they're a few kilometres west out along Highway 7.

Turn west toward the mountains, you can't miss them—I think."

"Thank you," I said, wondering how a true Okotokian could not know where the famous rocks were.

Sure enough we found them, right where she said they had last been spotted. There was a nice little tourist pullout and a swanky gravel trail leading up to the bungalow-sized boulders. Several tourists were walking, zombie-like, down the gravel path, as though the boulders possessed some supernatural magnetic force that was drawing them in for a closer look. We dutifully followed in line behind them.

I have to admit that, for a couple of boulders, they were rather impressive. Not if you saw them with other boulders, and not if you saw them in the Rockies, where rocks are rather easy to find. But here, sitting forlornly on the open, windswept prairie, abandoned by all their friends, they seemed clearly out of place, much like the large tourists ambling down the trail ahead of us.

Interpretive signs informed us (as interpretive signs are prone to do) that the boulders originated in the Jasper area and weighed in at 16,000 metric tonnes. A few people scrambled about the rocks like spiders, which seemed an obvious thing to do, other than just stand there stupidly staring at them, which is what we did.

"I wonder how many people a year come here and say, 'Wow. They're big, eh?'" I posed this question to no one in particular, mostly because no one in particular was standing beside me at the time.

We headed west along Highway 7, where we would soon hang south at Black Diamond onto . . . cue the western theme music . . . the Cowboy Trail.

Every highway nowadays has to have a special name, or so goes the theory of tourism marketing that states "If you name your highway something, innocent schmucks will travel enormous distances out of their way and part with their hard-earned dollars by stopping at gift shops to buy bumper stickers that read 'I Drove the Decapitated Gopher Scenic Parkway.'"

I guess it makes a bit of sense. I mean, who wants to trundle along a highway named after a number when you could be moseying on down the Cowboy Trail? Alberta has embraced this naming craze, giving us not only the Cowboy Trail, but the Red Coat Trail, the Buffalo Trail, the Grizzly Trail, the Hoo Doo Trail, and the There's Not a Damn Thing to See on This Here Trail Trail (also known as Highway 2 between Edmonton and Calgary).

As names go, the Cowboy Trail seems the most appropriate for western Alberta. It makes you feel as though at any moment you might be attacked by a gang of black-masked rum-running bandits or, at the very least, tailgated by an SUV-driving cowboy in a hurry to get back to his sprawling hobby ranch. At least we got to experience the latter.

We stopped briefly at the information centre/coffee shop at Black Diamond. This quaint little town just screams out "I'm a quaint little town, damn it!" This is the kind of town where you would expect to run into a real cowboy, not one of those fake cowboys you find at the Calgary Stampede, but a *real* cowboy, complete with boots and Stetson and maybe even a horse. Alas, we found only fellow tourists, including a couple of Brits who thought *I* was a real cowboy. Boy, were they confused.

Had the draw from a hat played out differently, Black Diamond would have been named Arnoldville, after the Arnold brothers, who ran the first general store here. Fortunately, a name suggested by rancher Addison McPherson for his local mine, the Black Diamond Coal Mine, won the draw. I say "fortunately" because, to me, Arnoldville conjures up the image of a place where one might find a bunch of Arnolds, and I was in no mood for that.

We did find a burger joint in Black Diamond that claimed to serve world-famous peanut butter burgers. Mmmm, mmmm. Some foods make your stomach do cartwheels of joy . . . this was not one of those foods. I wondered what the locals thought of a peanut butter burger here in the heart of Alberta beef country. Sounds like a pansy sort of thing to do, slathering peanut butter all over your Alberta beef, doesn't it?

Still, I tried the world-famous peanut butter burger and have to confess that their claim of being world famous is probably accurate. In fact, I'm sure there is someone in a little bar in Bora Bora talking about this burger right now.

Moseying south along the Cowboy Trail, passing a sign advertising a "Horse Blanket Repair Shop," we knew we truly were on the trail of some real cowboys.

In twenty minutes we pulled into Longview, another western town with a western feel to it. In fact, everyone we saw was wearing a cowboy hat—even the dogs. This is Ian Tyson country, which made it feel even more cowboyish. We looked for Ian in his cozy little coffee shop, the Navajo Mug, but found only Bob.

Longview is also the locale of the pivotal bar scene in the 1992 movie *Unforgiven*, wherein Clint Eastwood tells Gene Hackman, "Go ahead, make my day." Perhaps that was another movie he said that in—the important point of this aside is that Clint was here, which boosts the place even higher on the old cowboy meter.

Just south of Longview, we found the mini-tourist attraction we were looking for—the famous baseball cap fence, where each fence post is beautifully adorned with a baseball cap. The baseball-capped fence was created by rancher Lorne

The best-dressed fence in the west.

Fuller, who, of course, owns the fence and who obviously has a great sense of humour. Either that or a bizarre fetish for baseball caps.

I believe that this is not merely any old baseball cap fence, but the *largest* baseball cap fence in the entire world. (It's got to be, I mean, we're talking Alberta here, right?) The fence, on the west side of the highway, stretches almost two kilometres. We pulled off the road to examine it more closely and found caps from all over the world nailed to the posts. There were also other donations to the cause—plastic bags draped over a couple of posts, each crammed full to the brim with assorted used baseball caps.

Feeling as though we should make a contribution, I sacrificed my favourite baseball cap to the cause. (Okay, so it was my twelfth favourite, but it would have been my favourite if not for the other eleven caps I like better.)

Fifteen kilometres south of Longview we paid a visit to the Bar U National Historic Ranch, where we learned that at one time you could purchase ranchlands in these parts for a cent an acre.

"Why do we always seem to miss out on all the great deals?" my wife pined. Indeed, hailing from Canmore, where you need half a million for a storage shed, we found this fact a tad depressing.

After chatting up a few of the horses at the Bar U, we hung east onto a gravel road—Highway 540—which would take us back over to Highway 2. Kicking up a storm of dust made us feel even more Albertan.

"Aren't you feeling more Albertanish, honey?" I asked my wife. Had she been able to respond through all her choking and coughing, I'm sure she would have agreed.

Halfway to Highway 2, the gravel morphed into pavement, and we quickly discovered that we had found what would likely claim the Most Potholed Highway in Alberta award. This was the only highway I'd seen that came with its own built-in rumble strips. We were dodging potholes the size of Pavarotti's bathtub. As I gripped the steering wheel, I was instantly transformed into Han Solo flying through that horrendous meteor shower, yelling to my wife (playing the role of Princess Leia), "Never tell me the odds!"

"Boy, it takes a keen eye to hit every single pothole," my wife said. Wives. Still so much fun to have on road trips.

We passed by what appeared to be a gopher cemetery, featuring about three dozen flattened ground squirrels along a 200-metre stretch of road. It was like one of those elephant cemeteries you read about, where elephants go to die, only, well, with gophers instead of elephants. (Question: How many dead gophers does it take before one of them stands at the side of the road assessing all the carnage and says to himself, "Maybe this isn't such a good idea after all"?)

More cows. More sheep. More wind. A sign welcoming "Experienced Shooters." And a directional sign to a Hutterite colony.

"How many Hutterites does it take to change a light bulb?" I asked my wife.

Had she been awake, I'm sure she would have laughed.

It was thirty-five degrees out by the time we turned south, back again onto Highway 2. The wind was howling like a wolf in heat, the sky a brilliant summer blue—a classic southern Alberta summer day.

The billboard announcing our imminent arrival to Nanton screamed out "Where History Lives!"

"There must be a lot of old people in Nanton," my wife said.

We passed by Nanton's Double D Motel, a place where Dolly Parton might feel right at home, and the Lancaster Bomber on display at Nanton's air museum. But what really caught my eye was a sign boasting "Home of Canada's Largest Garden Railway." Now *this* was something I had to see.

Owing to the generous travel budget my publisher had arranged for this trip, my wife decided to opt out of paying the three-dollar admission fee to the garden railway, situated at the back of the garden railway building. The entrance was guarded by a miniature collie, giving the impression that everything would be in miniature form.

Out in the garden, I stood beside eight retired folks, all lined up in a row, hands plunged deep into front pockets (which, I've noticed, seems to be the pose of choice for retired people watching something). Laid out before us was the garden railway, snaking its way around miniature villages, trees, mountains, and grain elevators. One train was a replica of an Amtrak train that, owing to the wind, derailed right in front of us.

"Interesting it was only the Amtrak train that derailed, don't you think?" I asked one of the old-timers. He looked over at me grimly, with a look that suggested I was obviously an outsider who knew nothing of the day-to-day realities and stresses associated with the running of a garden railway.

Watching the trains chug on by, I kept waiting—truth be told, hoping—for King Kong to make an appearance and terrorize the trains' tiny little passengers. Alas, there was no King Kong, not even a simulation of an earthquake.

Back inside the shop, my investigative sidekick discovered that a write-in campaign had been started by the shop, urging its patrons to write in about Nanton's garden train so it could be featured in *Garden Train* magazine.

"Doesn't it seem odd that Canada's largest garden train has not made it into *Garden Train* magazine?" I asked my wife.

"Doesn't it seem odd that there is a magazine devoted to garden trains?" she responded. She had me there.

Back on the highway, we passed Stavely, one of those tiny prairie popup towns sitting just far enough off the highway that you have to actually want to go there to see it. Its welcome sign proudly declared "Stavely—Home of Canada's First Indoor Rodeo." Is this really something to brag about? Aren't rodeos an obvious thing to hold outdoors? Doesn't it get smelly in there? Don't the cowboys sometimes get thrown into the roof? So many questions, so little time. Stavely would have to wait. We needed to press on to make it to Head-Smashed-In Buffalo Jump before closing.

Within an hour, we were pulling into the parking lot at Head-Smashed-In Buffalo Jump, a World Heritage Site and one of the windiest places in the known galaxy. It was so windy that my hat blew off my head. Is that windy or *what?*

Head-Smashed-In, or as I've heard some visitors refer to it, Mashed-in-Dead or Smashed-in-the-Head, is truly one of the most remarkable historical sites anywhere in Canada. The place never fails to impress me. Built right into the cliff, the interpretive centre looks like the kind of place where Batman or James Bond's evil nemesis might hang out.

As is typical during the peak season, the place was swarming with bus tours, children's groups, and the odd (very odd, truth be told) random tourists. An introductory film introduces visitors to the site, while numerous dioramas explore the area's historical and ecological significance. At the top of the centre, a short trail leads visitors to a viewpoint along the edge of the cliff, providing a panoramic view of the prairies and the actual site where the buffalo were driven over the cliff by Blackfoot hunters.

I'd always assumed that the name Head-Smashed-In referred to the smashed-in heads of the buffalo. The real story is that the site is named for some doofus who, trying to get a front-row seat to the action from below the cliff, got his head smashed in by the falling buffalo. Let this be a lesson to all of us: never stand below a cliff where massive herds of buffalo are dropping over the edge.

I chatted with a few employees and asked if anything humorous ever happened here.

"Only when visitors drop by," deadpanned one.

They did share a few stories. For example, the time a woman refused to get off the tour bus for fear of being attacked by hostile Indians. (I really hope the information attendant was making that one up.) They also shared a few of their favourite silly tourist questions:

"Are you a *real* Indian?"

"Where are your teepees?"

"Where do you hide your bearskins?"

"When do the buffalo jump?"

"Are we too late for the buffalo jump?"

"Has the last buffalo jumped yet?"

"When's the next jump?"

"Are the jumps hourly?"

Sensing a recurring theme, I figured it was time to hit the open road again.

?

The wind had picked up even more. As we sailed through historic Fort Macleod, southern Alberta's oldest settlement, I wondered how history could have possibly got a toehold here with all the wind. I mean, how could anything or anyone have settled here?

"They probably pegged down their tents properly," my wife said, alluding to some incident from our past that I'd really rather not get into right now.

Deciding to make a quick dash to the BC border to investigate a few goofy roadside attractions, we headed west along Highway 3. Passing by the surreal, futuristic-looking wind turbines that dot the landscape, I recalled the story of a tourist who believed the turbines were there to *create* wind, which is, of course, a ridiculous notion if you've ever spent time in southern Alberta. The place tends to be a tad windy from time to time. Which is sort of like saying Saskatchewan tends to be a tad flat. In fact, the area is so windy, I'm told, that after three days of constant wind, many folks feel like killing one another for annoying indiscretions such as breathing or, say, showing up at a designated time and place.

The first offbeat attraction awaited us at Pincher Creek, named because someone from a surveying party way back when left behind a pair of pincers (a kind of gripping tool) near the creek. In honour of this monumental event, Pincher Creek has erected a giant pair of pincers. The pincers, some 4 metres high, are just off the main street. As far as giant pincers go, they are quite impressive, but please keep in mind that I've never seen pincers before, let alone giant ones, so maybe I'm not the best person to ask.

Driving through downtown Pincher Creek, it was clear by the pincer symbols showing up on light posts that Pincher Creek had embraced its pincer theme. (Let's all be thankful the forgetful fellow didn't leave behind a pair of toenail clippers.)

Pincher Creek's famed giant pincers, not to be confused with giant pliers, tweezers, or forceps.

Back on the Number 3, we passed by the Frank Slide. Here, many a visitor has been known to comment, "It sure is fortunate the slide stopped at the highway. Imagine how many more people could have been killed!"

At the wee town of Bellevue, we pulled in by the giant crows to have a quick look at its smallest church. This particular wee church seemed no smaller than Drumheller's wee church, offering room for about eight wee little souls. The guest book recorded entries, most from Albertans, with about seventy-five entries saying "Cute" and another twenty or so from members of the state-the-obvious club: "Small church." Thanks for the insight, folks.

As we drove to Coleman, the radio announcer offered the definitive, 100 percent safe weather forecast for Alberta: "Depending on where you are right now, it's either sunny, cloudy, or raining." Add snow, and I think this guy's on to something big here.

At Coleman, we got lost looking for the "World's Largest

Piggy Bank," which, owing to the town's size, is difficult to do. The piggy bank turned out to be a railroad car known as 10-Ton Toots. The front was painted with a pig's face. Along the side, there was a slot where you could deposit money to help support community projects, such as more piggy banks that would capture even more money for more community projects.

?

After reaching the BC border in the Crowsnest Pass and failing to find a "Welcome to BC" sign (thus failing to feel properly welcomed), we backtracked along Highway 3 to Fort Macleod, hanging south onto Highway 2 toward Stand Off. Blowing canola fields, windswept cows leaning in the wind, a sign saying "Bridge for Sale," and soon Chief Mountain was rising in the distance. Now *this* felt like the deep Alberta south.

"10-Ton Toots."

We made our way to Woolford Provincial Park, one of those provincial parks the province evidently doesn't want you to find out about. I'm not saying that just because it was off two minor highways and at the end of a gravel road. I'm saying that because, despite having to make about four turns to find it, there was not a single directional sign to be found. That might explain why we had the entire campground to ourselves.

Day 2

After a restful night at our very own campground, we got an early start and headed for Cardston. The tourist sign at the town entrance featured the usual tourist symbols, with one notable exception: a symbol that looked remarkably like King Kong's head.

We followed King Kong's head (how could you not?) and found the attraction. It was the Fay Wray memorial fountain. Fay Wray, the actress who played the damsel in distress in the original 1933 *King Kong* flick, was born on a ranch southwest of Cardston. The fountain, which had obviously seen better days, commemorated Fay's visit back home in 1962, during Cardston's sixtieth anniversary. The fountain featured an interpretive panel and a silhouette of Kong himself. Yes, King Kong was in the heart of Mormon country.

We cruised the streets of Cardston, marvelling most not at the beautiful old homes, nor at the impressive Latter-day Saints temple, but at the width of the streets. The roads get wider, I had astutely noticed, the farther south one travels in Alberta. And these roads were among the widest I had seen—you could pull a U-turn in a motorhome on these babies. The streets were so wide, I imagined that even the most athletic of gophers wouldn't dare to cross them.

We spent two hours exploring the Remington Carriage Museum, Cardston's premier tourist attraction and a site that had recently earned the honour of Canada's Best Indoor Attraction. There was no King Kong at the museum, but there were a lot of carriages. And when I say "a lot of carriages," I mean it in the same way someone might casually comment, "Boy, there are a lot of tourists in Banff." With more than 215 carriages on display, this was carriage central.

The museum was founded by a fellow named Remington, who, rumour has it, went a little buggy trying to amass the world's greatest collection of carriages. A little buggy. Oh my gosh, the fun doesn't stop in southern Alberta, not even in Cardston.

We looped eastward south of Cardston along lonely, but scenic (in a lonely sort of way) Highway 501 toward Del Bonita. Lots of cows, lots of ground squirrels, very few cars and, near Atena (named for the famous volcano Mt. Etna), a sign advertising "Custom Semen Collection Service. Visitors Welcome." (I mused about stopping, suggesting to my wife that perhaps I could earn a little extra spending money for the trip ahead, but she declined my generous offer.)

We blinked past Del Bonita, then nipped south to the border crossing, which was eerily quiet. Noting all the words I should probably avoid saying—like "terrorist," "bomb," or "fiduciary" (because I'm not totally sure how to pronounce it)—I cautiously entered the Canada Customs building. A lone guard greeted me in a part friendly, part "What the hell are you doing in the middle of nowhere walking into our office, and are you a threat to our sovereign nation?" kind of way.

I gave her a broad, warm Albertan smile and held up my hands in a "Hey, look at me, I'm a nice guy" kind of gesture, which made her immediately reach for her sidearm. After we cleared things up, and I had a chance to explain that I was merely a tourist and humble author researching a goofy book, she looked at me even more suspiciously.

"There's nothing funny about Albertans," she said flatly.

"Well, you probably don't see them at their best," I suggested. "You know, strip searches tend to be a little off-putting to the best of us."

"What's this book about?" she asked.

"I have no idea until it's done"—an answer that seemed to confuse both her and my publisher.

"Funny stuff, huh?" she said. "Well, there was that time I terrorized that retired couple from Lethbridge after they failed to declare a package of gum they bought in Arizona. Do you mean those kinds of stories?"

"You know, humour is a very subjective thing," I replied, trying to ease my way out the door.

"Okay, well, it's not as funny, but I do get asked questions like 'Do you know my cousin in Winnipeg?'"

"That's kind of funny."

"Or, 'Do you know the guys on the other side?'"

"That's great," I replied.

"Or, 'How far is it to Leatherbridge?'"

"Good one."

"So will these make it into your book?"

"Will I get a free pass to cross the border back and forth as I please for the rest of my life?"

With that, the interview was (rather abruptly) over.

Heading east again along Highway 501, a.k.a. the No One Ever Drives This Scenic Trail Trail. More cows, more ground squirrels. Many, many more ground squirrels. Why do ground squirrels so often run out to the centre of the highway, stop, and then rise onto their hind legs to look around? What are they looking for—death? Is it a dare? Do they want to see if there's enough clearance to make it under the vehicle even if they're standing? Because, let me go on record right now as saying there's not.

Passing along so close to the U.S. border, I recalled reading how Montana cows used to sneak across the border to graze and then sneak on back home to their own turf. Of course, they probably had help. Still, it bothered me that cows could be so sneaky. Somehow, I always thought of them as being rather noble creatures.

We hit the town of Milk River at noon and, lucky for us, the Canada Day celebration at the Milk River Alberta Travel Visitor Information Centre. This meant one thing: free doughnuts. Oh Canada!

"Did you know that Canadians consume more doughnuts than anywhere on the planet?" I said, stuffing another honey-glazed cruller into my mouth.

"No kidding," my wife replied.

We posed in front of the scary giant dinosaur that guards the entrance to the centre, then left for our final destination of the day, Writing-on-Stone Provincial Park.

Writing-On-Stone is one of my favourite spots in Alberta, a true geological and historical wonder. And here's one of the many things I wondered about as we pulled into our campsite: why were people sitting around a roaring campfire during the middle of a sweltering thirty-eight degree day?

We wandered down to the beach along the Milk River, and I immediately noticed I was the only person wearing a thong, so I quickly excused myself. After slipping into something a little more comfortable, I made three floats down the river on an inner tube, which seems to be the predominant way folks appreciate the area's historical significance.

Strolling through the campground later that afternoon, we walked past a campsite that was entirely consumed by the largest motorhome I'd ever seen. The mammoth beast, outfitted with a satellite dish and a rather noisy generator, looked like it had taken out two or three trees in the process of settling snugly into its berth. The name splashed along the side (and I'm not making this up) was, oh-so appropriately enough, The Intruder.

Spying another motorhome with the name Swinger, we began wondering just what sort of campground this was. Fortunately, we ran into a couple of bunnies and a few deer and somehow felt safer.

Heading out on the main hiking trail, which passes by stunning vistas of the river valley and through fascinating geological formations, we ended up at a site where you can view some of the park's famed petroglyphs.

The petroglyphs are protected by a fence—this is a good thing. We could make out the crude markings of animals, people, and a message that read "Linda Loves Patrick." Hopefully Linda is in jail right now, because the sign on the fence warns visitors that there is a $50,000 fine or one-year jail sentence for defacing this archaeological treasure. And hopefully Patrick has long since left Linda, finally realizing what an incredible idiot she is.

Day 3

Up bright and early, we pulled out of rattlesnake country and were cruising the streets of Milk River by 8:00 AM. Again we noticed the wide streets, and a lonely, sad-looking dog waiting patiently for the liquor store to open. We passed by a display that includes all the flags of all the nations that have ruled the area, wondering where the First Nations flags were. (Boy, can I provide some biting commentary or what?)

After our tour of Milk River, completed in two minutes and thirty-six seconds (my wife kindly timed it), we headed north to Raymond. Yet again, wide, wide streets welcomed us. I had read a promo blurb somewhere that touted the "wide streets of Raymond" as a good reason to visit. The streets certainly facilitated easy U-turns, and my fear of a head-on collision was greatly diminished while touring Raymond, but somehow I felt that wide streets alone weren't enough of a draw for people to come off the highway. Perhaps they needed to learn from northern Alberta and erect a giant food item.

Raymond was the location of the first rodeo in western Canada. I comment on this only because it makes me look like I've done a lot of serious research on your behalf. What Raymond was *not* the site of was an open coffee shop, so we headed east.

By 9:00 AM, we were on the Red Coat Trail—Highway 61—which cuts an east-west swath across southern Alberta between Stirling and Manyberries. Sadly, the Red Coat Trail may have been more aptly named Can You Identify the Dead Animal in the Middle of the Road? Trail.

By the time we cruised into Foremost, my coffee-deprived body was screaming out what coffee-deprived bodies tend to scream out: "For God's sake, where's my coffee?" Coffee did not seem to be foremost in anyone's mind in Foremost, so I popped into the wee little tourist centre to ask for directions to the nearest coffee pot.

Two girls looked up at me as though I were an alien life form. Their deer-in-the-headlights expression suggested that perhaps I'd interrupted an armed robbery in progress, or possibly I had some strange foreign appendage growing out of the side of my face. A few awkward moments of silence passed before one of the girls explained they had just opened. In fact, this was day one of the Foremost Information Centre, and I was their very first tourist. They seemed fearful I might actually ask them a question, so I stalled for time to help ease their nerves.

"Wow, first! Do I win something?"

Shocked looks passed between them, as though I was already pointing out something critical they had overlooked.

"It's okay, really. I don't want anything, except a cup of good coffee."

"Coffee?"

"Exactly. Is there a coffee shop nearby?"

"There's Wong's Chinese restaurant, but I don't think they're open yet."

"Oh." Desperation was kicking in.

Fortunately they guided me back down the road to a restaurant we'd passed, where, indeed, they were brewing up some fresh, soul-warming coffee.

Everyone we drove past in Foremost waved at us, which is something you don't see in, say, just to offer an example, oh, I don't know . . . Calgary. At least not *this* kind of hand waving. This appeared to be a genuinely friendly and welcoming kind of hand waving, something we were not remotely accustomed to.

"What should I do?" I asked my wife.

"Wave back, you idiot," she so helpfully suggested.

As we pulled into Etzikom, a Calgarian was being interviewed on the radio about his plans to open a broom museum at the University of Michigan. This got me thinking about how there is a museum for everything these days, just as we pulled into the parking lot of Etzikom's windmill museum.

An interpretive panel introducing the exhibits included a quote by historian Walter J. Webb. "It was not the gun that settled the west, but the windmill." Settling things by windmills instead of guns—is that Canadian or what?

The windmill museum features fifteen different styles of windmills, from the Hummer to the Dempster self-oiling model, which sounded like the kind I'd enjoy, because, let's be honest, no one wants to spend their weekends oiling the damn windmill.

Pulling out of Etzikom, I smiled at the sight of an old man driving a golf cart down the main street. The ability to motor about in a golf cart was another attractive feature, I imagined, of life in a small town.

The highway got lonelier the farther east we went. The only moving vehicle we passed on our way to Orion was an old man, in the middle of nowhere, riding a bicycle that appeared to be about a century old. I imagine that both the Etzikom guy driving the golf cart and the fellow riding his bike are probably well known in these parts, and I bet you anything the local kids refer to them as "The Old Guy Who Drives his Golf Cart Everywhere" and "The Old Guy Who Rides His Bike Everywhere." I can't prove it, of course, but I'm almost certain those must be their nicknames.

Past the tiny town of Orion, then Manyberries, we turned south along Highway 889. Stepping out of the car to suck in some fresh southern Alberta air, we couldn't help but feel very, very small. And very alone. Puffy white clouds formed the shape of a grizzly bear sow nuzzling her cub—unless you're my wife, who saw Brad Pitt riding naked atop a camel. Clearly we weren't looking at the same cloud.

Back in the car, we soon came upon gravel roads as we wound our way through Onefour, home of the world's largest dinosaur turd. The discovery of the fossilized, 75 million-year-old *Tyrannosaurus rex* poop, known as a coprolite, meant that Saskatchewan could no longer claim the title as home to the world's largest dinosaur poop, which made me feel very proud to be an Albertan. There were no signs or museums touting this fabulous find—an obviously overlooked tourist gold mine.

We decided to camp in Cypress Hills, Alberta's only inter-provincial park. We thought briefly about camping on the Saskatchewan side, but then we'd be in Saskatchewan, which would defeat the purpose of an Albertan road trip. So we headed for Elkwater, where, at the gas station, they have a hitch for your dog and a "barking lot." Is that ridiculously cute, or what?

The park's summer resort of Elkwater is the weekend destination of choice for overheated Medicine Hatters and Saskatchewan folks looking for a little fun in the water. The beach was covered in white-bodied humanoids of various shapes and sizes; the lake teemed with jet skiers, water skiers, boaters, and swimmers.

The Cypress Hills that surround Elkwater are the highest point of land between the Rockies and Labrador, a pretty oasis of gently rolling hills and forests surrounded by a sea of prairies. "Cypress" is a misnomer. The hills were named by some French explorers who thought the trees they were seeing were cypress, which they are not.

"You can't trust the French to get things right," I said to my wife.

"I'm French," she reminded me, shooting me a look that informed me you can indeed trust the French.

I decided to change the subject. "It's a pretty area."

"Yes," she replied. "Just like the Rockies, only without that annoying scenery and majestic grandeur."

Wandering through the campsite before supper, we came upon the oddest sighting. Someone had pitched their tent on the side of a hill, such that it was easily at a forty-five degree slope. I had never seen such a thing. Either these were new campers who hadn't been advised that finding a flat patch of property is one of the most important parts of camping, or they enjoyed waking up with 90 percent of their blood pooled in their feet.

As I watched my wife cut wood, fetch water, start the fire, pitch the tent, make dinner, then do the dishes, I sat in my camp chair musing about how incredibly relaxing camping can be. It was a gorgeous night for stargazing, so we sat out until nightfall, listening intently to the sounds of Mother Nature. On this particular evening, that included the hum of a sick generator, a loud and somewhat obnoxious drunk, and a ghetto blaster screaming out a pounding rock tune. Ah, nature at its best.

Now allow me to go on record right now as saying this: if there is one crime worthy of the death penalty, it is the crime of making annoying noises in a campground at night on beautiful starry evenings. These are the people who we cannot simply wait for evolution to take care of. Somebody has to intervene.

Day 4

The road trip swung north along Highway 41—the Buffalo Trail. There were no buffalo, but there were some humping cows, which is always a nice substitute.

A sign let us know we were entering snake country: "Rattlesnakes are at risk. Watch for snakes next 50 km." As a huge fan of snakes, I was grateful for the sign. But having read a study once wherein researchers placed rubber snakes on a road to gauge motorists' reactions, I was slightly pessimistic about the chances for their survival along this stretch of highway. In the study, most motorists swerved to hit the fake snake, some backed up once or twice, while a few, as I recall, even turned around to make sure they finished the job. Hopefully we've progressed a little. (The fact that Lethbridge is introducing rattlesnake crossings and relocating some snakes within city limits makes me think we're on the right track.)

We got as far as the South Saskatchewan River Valley, an absolutely gorgeous river valley, before stopping for a snack at a picnic site. It was approximately 147 degrees out, so we ate as fast as we could and turned back for Medicine Hat.

At Medicine Hat, we ventured into the world's largest teepee, then popped into the Medicine Hat Information Centre. Outside the centre sat David's Weather Stone, which claimed to predict the weather with 100 percent accuracy using the following technique:

If the rock is wet . . . it's raining.
If the rock is white . . . it's snowing.
If the rock is moving back and forth . . . it's windy.
If it's hard to see . . . it's foggy.
If it's casting a shadow . . . it's sunny.
If it's cold . . . it's cold out.
If it's hot . . . it's hot out.

If only we could get meteorologists with this kind of intelligence.

Back along Highway 3, headed for home now. Eighteen kilometres southeast of Medicine Hat, we stopped in at Seven Persons, a small town that offers a couple possible origins for its name, both involving sixteen people, but with the metric conversion, it became seven.

The first version refers to a battle in which seven Cree men were killed by Blood hunters at a nearby creek. The second version is the far more interesting one, so it must be the real version. A band of Blackfoot hunters happened upon seven dead and hairless, but not scalped, men. Bewildered, the Blackfoot men watched the bodies for five days, concluding they must have been struck down by the Great Spirit. So they erected a burial cairn, but when they returned next spring . . . the bodies were gone.

This sort of phenomenon I would expect from southeastern Alberta. After all, there have been many UFO sightings around here, not to mention some weird circular depressions that could only have been made by aliens. Or bored teenagers.

We popped into Premium Sausage, the hotspot of Seven Persons, which served triple duty as general store and town post office. This family-run business won my heart for three reasons. First, they had a guest book, and a quick scan of the entries revealed that most of the population of Seven Persons had actually signed the thing. How great is that? Second, they flew both the Canadian and Albertan flags on their building, something I'd rarely seen during any of my Alberta travels. Finally, they still had a place you could hitch up your horse to.

Twenty-four kilometres south of Seven Persons, we sat in awe at a picnic table overlooking the Red Rock Coulee Natural Area. The table was chained to the ground, making us conclude that picnic table thievery was an issue around these parts. But that's not why we were in awe.

Our amazement was due to the spectacularly unique and beautiful coulee before us. It was a barren landscape, save for the odd patch of sage or cactus, and for the star attraction: large red rocks, all roughly the same size, all roughly the same shape.

We scrambled down a trail to inspect the rocks. The landscape was dotted with these round boulders, as high as my chest, about 2 metres across. Most had flat tops, as if the top had been neatly sliced off. The area looked like a giant abandoned ceramics shop.

Abandoned, of course, by aliens. Teenagers couldn't have pulled this one off.

?

We rolled into Bow Island, the "Bean Capital of the West," which made me wonder if there was a bean capital of the east. The town slogan explained the presence of the giant town mascot greeting travellers from the east—Pinto McBean—but did little to explain the presence of the "World's Largest Golf Putter."

Bow Island is also the "Sunflower Seed Capital of Canada." This explained the many signs saying things like "Have you fed your bird today?"

Wow, this place was a gold mine! Home to the world's largest golf putter, the bean capital of the west, and the sunflower seed capital of Canada—all in one little town on the prairie. I hardly knew where to begin, so I strolled into the tourist information trailer beside Pinto McBean and was promptly rewarded with two free bags of sunflower seeds. This truly was the sunflower seed capital of Canada!

Pinto McBean stands guard over the "Bean Capital of the West."

After lunch, which, sadly, featured neither beans nor sunflower seeds, we headed west, stopping at the town of Burdett, "Home of the First Irrigation Pivot in Canada!" It was exciting to learn that Burdett, Alberta, was the site, way back on 11 May, 1962, of the arrival of the first pivot irrigation system in Canada. But not nearly as exciting to find out that J Lo herself, Jennifer Lopez (who, at the time of this trip, might or might not have been marrying actor Ben Affleck), was in town working on a film.

I tried to track her down, just for the sake of research. I wanted to ask what Miss Hotshot Hollywood thought of southern Alberta, and also to find out when her impending on-again-off-again marriage to Ben Affleck might be taking place, and if I would be invited to the wedding.

After being escorted out of town by two bodyguards for Ms. Lopez (who, in my books, throws around words like "stalker" rather loosely), we continued westward.

Somewhere along this stretch of Highway 3, my wife got very upset with me for picking a piece of muffin off the car floor and eating it. I include this to prove to you that I believe in fully disclosing the truth, even when the truth isn't very pretty.

Having consumed copious quantities of its famous corn (as my wife, who has an ear for all things corn, said, "Taber has *corn*ered the market on corn"), I was excited about our imminent arrival at Taber.

We paused long enough for a photo op at a giant stalk of corn, then headed into the Taber museum. Like the info centre in Foremost, the staff looked a little frightened, so we bypassed asking them any questions and meandered on into the small museum. We learned that in 1999 the Taber Hostess Plant (as in Hostess potato chips) was rated the number one Hostess plant in western Canada and the western US. (This is the kind of trivia that a trivia nut like me will happily squirrel away with all the other nuts of information I've cached, just waiting for the perfect time to spring it on some unsuspecting chip eater.) The display even featured three bags of potato chips: barbecue, salt n' vinegar, and regular, just in case you forgot what bags of potato chips look like.

At the gift shop there were flyswatters for sale, boasting that the official hummingbird of Taber was the mosquito. Those crazy kidders. I was beginning to love Taber, and also starting to crave potato chips.

We stopped at Kirk's Uniroyal Toyo Shop to check out the

statue of a giant woman that lords over the parking lot. Upon close examination, the woman looked to me to be a man in drag. She (he?) had a come-hither look, so obviously the statue was intended to lure unsuspecting male motorists into the tire shop. In fact, the longer I stared at her (him?), the more she (he?) seemed to be saying "Come on in, big boy, I'll rotate your tires."

?

North along Highway 36, headed now for Vauxhall (named for a London suburb), home of course to Sammy and Samantha Vauxhall. Sammy and Samantha are legendary pillars of the Vauxhall community, a couple whose feet are firmly planted on the ground, in reinforced concrete. They're a pair of giant,

Taber's giant cross-dresser.

very happy potatoes, among the happiest potatoes I've ever met, whose role is to welcome travellers to the "Potato Capital of the West."

Vauxhall had a very southern Albertan farm community feel to it, complete with wide streets.

"Doesn't it feel farmish here?" I asked my wife.

"Is 'farmish' a word?" she asked me back.

"Of course," I replied.

Wives. Still fun to have along. Even on day four.

As we headed west now along Highway 526 to Enchant, it was clear we were in real agriculture country, complete with real farms and real crops and everything. Our thirty-six-second tour through "enchanting" Enchant revealed quite possibly the widest streets of the trip thus far, a road girth that rivaled even Raymond.

Although only a wee hamlet, Enchant still had its own golf course. Even the smallest towns we encountered had their own golf course, which says something about something, doesn't it? I mean, it must.

Picture Butte claimed to be the "Livestock Feed Capital of Canada." This seemed a tad incongruent with its charming name. I somehow imagine that the slogan doesn't lure a lot of tour bus traffic off the main highways.

We passed by Diamond City, which seemed to have a total of about fifteen homes, so really its claim of being a city seems a little unjustified. I made a mental note to bring that up with them the next time I'm through the area.

At Nobleford, we strolled through the historic farm equipment park, answering the question "How can you tell you're in southern Alberta?" rather nicely. Nobleford's claim to fame is being "Home of the Noble Blade," a type of cultivating farm blade invented by the village's original pioneer, Charles Sherwood Noble. Mr. Noble reportedly started farming the hard way—by walking barefoot behind an ox team. A true Albertan, that Charles Noble.

As predicted, as we headed north along Highway 23, past Barons, the "Wheat Heart of the West," the streets became less and less wide.

The town of Champion bills itself as the "Gateway to Little Bow Provincial Park." This seemed, to be brutally honest, like not the greatest claim to fame. First of all, "gateway" communities are always a little suspect. What being a gateway community says is this: "We have nothing neat to offer you, but we're really really close to something neat." That's why all over the world you'll find slogans like:

Sudbury, ON—Gateway to Newfoundland and Europe!

Surrey, BC—Gateway to Hawaii!

Welcome to the United States—Gateway to Canada!

My second concern with Champion's town slogan is that if you must be a gateway community, at least be a gateway to something truly amazing, like the Canadian Rockies, the Great Barrier Reef, or Mars. I mean no offence to the people of Champion, heck, I haven't even met you. Nor do I mean to offend Little Bow Provincial Park, because I really really like provincial parks. But come on—Gateway to Little Bow Provincial Park? This is sort of like saying "Surrey—Gateway to Richmond!"

Okay, now that I have that off my chest, we can get on with things. The trip is drawing to an end, and I really must get home anyway.

By nightfall we pulled into our driveway, having covered 1,847 kilometres on southern Albertan roads.

"Well, honey, do you feel more like a real Albertan now?"

"I could have felt more Albertan in Italy," she replied.

Wives. So much fun to have on road trips.

deep questions posed by tourists in alberta

When does Alberta close down?

Is Alberta a country yet?

If Alberta joined the United States, what would you be called and where would you be located?

Are all the roads in Alberta dirt roads?

You just recently began speaking English in Alberta, didn't you?

Is this the part of Canada where they speak a lot of French, or is that Saskatchewan?

western alien nation

Surprisingly, the rural town of Vulcan, southeast of Calgary, was *not* named for the home planet of Mr. Spock and countless other green-blooded Vulcans, but rather for the Roman god of fire and metalworking. Nonetheless, one can still find Vulcans in Vulcan, especially during Vulcan's annual *Star Trek* Galaxyfest convention.

The yearly convention, held since 1993, has proven to be a real bonanza for Vulcan. You see, when you're trying to figure out how to attract tourists to a small agricultural community, you need a gimmick. And if your town just happens to be named for the fictional home planet of a major pop culture icon, you've been handed a gigantic gimmick on a silver platter, or at least aboard a silver spaceship. Because if there is one subset of humans that will travel great distances to a place called Vulcan, it's those obsessive-compulsive, delightfully quirky *Star Trek* enthusiasts known as Trekkies.

I decided to make like a Trekkie and trek off into the final frontier of Alberta, to search out strange new worlds, to seek out new life and new civilizations, and maybe grab a burger along the way. Yes, I boldly went where no man has gone before (unless that man had a really good map, because Vulcan is a bit off the beaten path) to participate in Vulcan's annual *Star Trek* convention. (When I say "participate," what I really mean is "watch from a frightened distance.")

As I landed my Honda space shuttle in Vulcan (where signs welcomed me to this "friendly, earthly community"), I felt like Captain Kirk, Mr. Spock, and Dr. McCoy all rolled into one, conducting a landing-party recon mission on a strange foreign landscape. My inner Spock was saying, "Highly illogical, captain—a sci-fi theme in the middle of a rural Alberta agricultural community?" My inner Dr. McCoy was telling me, "Damn it, Jim, I'm a humorist, not a Trekkie," while my inner Kirk was saying, "Where will the cutest Trekkies be hanging out, and will their skirts be as short as in the original *Star Trek* series?"

Before emerging from my vehicle, I sampled the air (as any good intergalactic explorer would) and sucked in the sweet-smelling scent of Grade A Alberta manure. The incongruity of this alien landscape struck me as, well, rather incongruous. On the surface, Vulcan resembles one of those sleepy rural prairie towns that time, or at least the 1950s, forgot. Yet here, along the town's main street, sits a 9.5-metre-long replica of the *Starship Enterprise*, complete with a trilingual plaque welcoming visitors in English, Vulcan, and Klingon. The incongruity was nicely summed up in the town slogan: "From past to vast."

I cautiously entered the tourist Trek Station—Vulcan's spaceship-shaped tourist information centre—and quickly surmised that I was the only person at the convention attending as a civilian being from planet Earth. Talk about western alienation. The joint overflowed with Trekkies, mini-Trekkies, and Trekkie wannabes. Folks of all ages, shapes, and sizes

The Starship Enterprise double-parked outside the Vulcan information centre.

dressed up as assorted starship captains, Klingons, Borgs, Ferengies, Romulans, and, of course, Vulcans. A rocket-making contest was underway, there were trivia quizzes to test your knowledge (in which *Star Trek* episode did Captain Kirk say, "Someone beam me down some acting lessons—now, damn it!"?), a costume contest, a pet costume contest, and life-size cardboard cutouts of all the *Star Trek* captains standing aboard a replica of the *Starship Enterprise* bridge. There were guest speakers, *Star Trek* authors, make-up tips, and Klingon races, but sadly, no Klingon karaoke.

Thankfully, one could also purchase everything the aspiring Trekkie could ever want: space Slinkies, Vulcan ears, *Star Trek* gourmet coffee beans, small jugs of Vulcan air, Klingon corkscrews, *Star Trek* badges, *Star Trek* shot glasses, *Star Trek* snow globes (it's sort of sad to think they still have snow globes in the future), *Star Trek* mouse pads, *Star Trek* beer steins, a bag of Tribbles (as featured in the 1966 episode "The Trouble with Tribbles"), Vulcan spoons, Vulcan Frisbees, *Star Trek* T-shirts, a futuristic-looking Vulcan lamp, painted *Star Trek* rocks, *Star Trek* watches, *Star Trek* posters, and *Star Trek* collectors plates. To say hi to the folks back home, you could send a postcard from Vulcan, featuring the *Starship Enterprise* flying above a grain elevator and an official intergalactic greeting: "Welcome to the third planet from the sun, North American continent, Province of Alberta, County of Vulcan. Live long and prosper."

One of the Trekkies, nine-year-old Andrew Gallant, visiting from St. Albert, Alberta, obviously recognized me as a lost soul and kindly escorted me around the site. Dressed as a captain of the *Star Trek* federation, Andrew proved to be a veritable computer databank of Trek trivia, reeling off facts and figures with the grim intensity of a Klingon commander. When asked about his future career plans, Andrew first told me he would like to grow up to be an actor on a *Star Trek* series. Then, after a few moments of deep contemplation, he changed his mind: "No, by the time I grow up, intergalactic space travel will be the norm, so I would prefer to be the *real* captain of a *Star Trek* spaceship." Attaboy, Andrew—dream big. (I mean, look at what dreaming big did for Canada's greatest comedic actor, William Shatner.)

After being shot by several phasers (fortunately they were

The author (disguised as a civilian) with Star Fleet Captains Austin and Andrew Gallant, and Admiral Bel Iv Satir and Lieutenant Commander B'Onego Satir. Moments after this photo was shot, the Klingons attacked a local 7-11.

all set to "stun"), I ventured outside toward the replica of a *Star Trek* space shuttle, which sat in the Trek Station parking lot. A crowd of folks had gathered around it, including the winners of the costume contest—a couple of married Klingons from Calgary. The Klingons invited me to join them later in the convention hospitality suite. They would be serving up a traditional Klingon drink called Warnog, served as only a good Klingon host would—out of a fresh toilet bowl. Although intrigued (who wouldn't be?), I politely declined the offer and boldly struck out on foot to explore the streets of Vulcan.

It was only 5:00 PM on a Saturday afternoon in July, yet it seemed as though the town of some 1,700 earthlings was already getting ready to turn in for the night, offering a peaceful respite from the intergalactic mayhem I had left behind. I was pleased to see that the *Star Trek* motif had spilled over into the entire community. Directional signs featured the *Star Trek* insignia, while many storefront windows were adorned with paintings or cutouts of *Star Trek* characters. There were *Star Trek* murals on many walls, including one with a forlorn

Mr. Spock gazing out at an Alberta farming landscape, as though he was pining for the good ole days back on the Alberta homestead. Window posters advertised the upcoming Spock Days rodeo event, held every July in Vulcan. Hungry visitors could bite into a Spock Burger at the Burger Baron, chomp on Vulcan fries at the local truck stop, or sip on an Iced Captain Kirk or Spock Sling at the Cinnastop coffee shop. Although many businesses

GREETINGS
WELCOME
TO
VULCAN

THIRD PLANET FROM THE SUN,
NORTH AMERICAN CONTINENT,
PROVINCE OF ALBERTA,
COUNTY OF VULCAN

LIVE LONG AND PROSPER

VULCAN ASSOC. FOR SCIENCE & TREK
(V.A.S.T.)

embraced the *Star Trek* spirit, sadly, not all of them did. For example, the local funeral parlour seemed downright sombre.

As chance would have it, I bumped into a former mayor of the town who told me that there was once a bar called Spock's that drew in people from as far away as Vancouver, and even Europe.

"You know, we knew we needed a gimmick to draw in the tourists," the ex-mayor told me. "Where are you from?"

"I'm from Canmore," I proudly replied.

"Ah, Canmore. What's your gimmick?" he asked.

"Didn't you hear me? I'm from Canmore! We don't need any gimmick!" I said. "We're set in the most beautiful location in Canada, next door to Canada's most famous national park, on the border of Alberta's greatest outdoor playground!"

"Oh," he said, rather disappointedly, "it's too bad you don't have a gimmick."

After taking one more stroll down the main drag, I pulled out my cell phone, dramatically whipped open the cover, phoned the only Scot I know, and blurted out "Beam me up, Scotty!" Unfortunately, I had called the wrong number, and someone named Marge told me to piss off.

After a day of hard Trekking, it was clearly time to return to the mother ship in Canmore.

To honour Vulcan's commitment to the sci-fi genre, the town was awarded a SPACEY lifetime achievement award in 2003 by the Canadian television channel SPACE. Mayor Dave Mitchell accepted the alien award wearing his red *Star Trek* admiral's shirt and, of course, pointy Vulcan ears. Vulcan seems to be a most worthy recipient of the SPACEY. After all, how many town councils have their very own *Star Trek* uniforms?

On 1 August 2004, a Calgary couple exchanged wedding vows inside the Vulcan Trek Station in a ceremony that was truly out of this world. The bride, a member of the international Klingon Assault Group, as well as a number of the guests, wore assorted Trekkie outfits, and the wedding even included a Klingon honour guard.

Of course, the marriage officiate possessed a passing knowledge of the Klingon language, as evidenced when he so eloquently spoke the words "Vaj mamuvchuq cha'moj wa," which translates roughly into "Thus we join one to another, one becomes two."

an a-mazing experience in the pun capital of alberta

If you are looking for something a little off-beet and very corny (as in, nothing to do with beets, lots to do with corn), pop into the a-maize-ing Lacombe Corn Maze, a site that gets my vote as the pun capital of Alberta.

This wacky attraction invites you to "Get Lost!" . . . inside a giant maze cut through a field of corn. Yes, you'll feel just like Kevin Costner in *Field of Dreams* as you heed the whispering voices beckoning you deeper and deeper inside the bowels of the cornfield maze (only to discover that the whispering voices are coming from a Saskatchewan couple who disappeared three years ago, when the husband refused to ask for directions out of the maze).

Before succumbing to the whispering voices, I perused the guest book at the ticket booth, hoping to find some clues on how to survive the experience. Instead, I discovered that the real purpose of the maze, besides offering up a much-needed diversion along Highway 2, is to provide an outlet for frustrated punsters from around the world. Entry upon entry from folks as far afield (get it? as far a field!) as Australia, England, and Mexico revealed their inexplicable need to pun: "the corniest thing I've ever seen," "corn-some!" "cornfusing!" "I got stalked inside the maize," "be careful what you say because there's a lot of ears out there," and "a corny time was had by all."

Victor Hugo once mused, "The pun is the guano of the winged mind," a comment he obviously made after visiting the Lacombe cornfield maze. One person, demonstrating a

Howdy. Am I happy to be here or what?

completely guano-filled mind, even signed the guest book after the legendary baseball figure Ty Cobb. About the only signature that didn't include a pun was the eloquent entry that simply read "My brother smells."

Trying to shake the pundits' comments from my head, I paid my ad-missing fee and bravely entered the maize. Brave, not because of any concern about ending up hopelessly cornered inside the maze, but because of my unnatural fear of corn, which stems from dreams about being stalked by the Jolly Green Giant's sidekick, the Little Green Sprout. (By the way, as all punsters must so painfully point out, did you get all my puns? Pundits? Ad-missing? Maize? Corn-ered? Stems? Stalked? I'm like some sort of punning savant!)

The welcoming folks who own the maze told me that it takes most normal people about forty-five minutes to an hour to successfully navigate the largest phase of the maze, which includes a total of about 7.2 kilometres of trails. But did I mention yet that I'm not normal? And being not normal, I confidently told the five-year-old standing next to me that I would see him back at the starting point in about ten minutes. Owing to my incredible bat-like sense of direction, my extensive experience navigating the Plus 15s in downtown Calgary, and, most importantly of all, the absence of my wife on this outing, I entered the maze with all the corn-fidence (I'm sorry, it's like an infectious disease) of a prize-winning homing pigeon on steroids.

An hour later, my confidence began to ebb. You see, the whole navigating the maze thing seems simple enough on the surface. After all, if gerbils can do it, I said to myself, surely to goodness a reasonably intelligent and devilishly handsome individual like myself can jog around this human rat race in no time at all. But soon, as I wandered deeper into the jungle of corn, turning and twisting and circling left and right and then right and then left, I began longing for a pair of whiskers, or at least a nice chunk of cheese to lead me on.

The maze didn't offer up any cheese. It does, however, offer trivia questions at important junctions. If you knew the correct answer to assorted pop culture stumpers such as "What is Homer Simpson's wife's maiden name?" or "When did Minnie enter Mickey's life?" the answer key let you know whether you should turn right, turn left, go straight ahead, or just lie on the ground and sob like a baby. (I must say, I did notice that combining a directional challenge with trivia questions proved to be an especially fun bonding experience for the married couples.) Since I knew the answers to, well, none of the questions, the trivia guide served only as a useful distraction from worrying about spending my golden years amid a field of golden ears.

I struck off toward a bridge from which one could get an expansive view of the entire maze. This unfortunately only served to offer me definitive proof that I was completely and utterly lost, that I had seemingly entered the pages of a

Stephen King novel, that I needed my mommy. I finally appreciated the severity of my situation when I ran into some cast members of *Survivor*.

Of course, asking people for help, besides being embarrassing, was completely useless. You soon realize that most people are directionally challenged, for example, the couple that I met that was looking for washrooms in West Edmonton Mall. Still, every time I encountered someone, I couldn't help but do what they in turn were obviously doing, too: slowly size them up and down and try to assess whether they are stupider than you. Upon sizing them up and down, I concluded most people were indeed stupider than me (no offence, most people), which meant that in all likelihood, I would be celebrating my next birthday with a nice dinner of corn.

A small plane circled overhead, apparently appreciating the giant design the maze cuts through the corn. (This year's theme, much to the punsters' delight, was a giant Canadian loony.) Hoping to get the pilot's attention, I jumped up and down, waving my arms like a goose in heat, or, I suppose, like a loon inside a loon, which only served to make that same five-year-old kid I met at the entrance hightail it back to his parents.

Dazed and cornfused . . .

Having failed to attract the plane's attention, I decided to have some fun with the whole experience by hiding in the corn and scaring small children with rustling noises and the occasional demonic growl. Because, really, what's more fun than scaring small children? My gosh, they were so right when they said this could be a fun experience for the whole family!

When I started hearing the theme song from *Deliverance*, I knew it was time to get out of the corn. Relying on my keen sense of smell, I boldly struck off in a northeastern direction (like I knew which direction was northeast) and within only twenty minutes managed to return to the very same spot I had just left.

Forgoing my keen sense of smell, I decided to move onward making my directional choices based on the flip of a coin—I was out of the maze in less than three minutes. The five-year-old boy was waiting for me at the entrance, obviously wanting to gloat. I informed the wee lad that because I was doing research for a book project, I had chosen to walk every inch of the maze.

He didn't seem to buy the argument either.

gopher mania

Why did the Albertan cross the road?

To show the gopher it could actually be done.

Alberta has an official bird (great horned owl), mammal (bighorn sheep), tree (lodgepole pine), flower (wild rose), fish (bull trout), meat (beef), and soon, once the votes are tallied, an official fungus. Okay, so we don't really have an official meat, but if we did, it would clearly be beef (please refer to "Top Ten Ways to Become an Albertan" on page 12).

What I think Alberta *really* needs, however, is an official pest, an enemy the entire province can rally around. Alberta's *unofficial* pest is Ottawa, but that hardly counts because we can't really say it out loud or the Feds will pay even less of our hard-earned money back into our coffers.

So where does that leave us? The mosquito seems like an obvious choice for a pest, but, realistically, Manitoba can probably rally the anti-mosquito forces far more eagerly and effectively than we could. So let's all agree that Manitoba can have the mosquito, okay?

The rat? Well, as I've already noted, we have no rats in the province. Why have an official pest if you can't at least visit it from time to time?

The only obvious choice, alas, falls on the wee little furry shoulders of our friend the gopher. (I know, it seems sort of mean designating a friend as the official pest. Oh well, someone has to take the fall, and it sure as heck isn't going to be me.)

Although most Albertans refer to anything small, furry, and rodent-like (including Joe Clark) as a gopher, chances are what they are seeing/feeding/running over is not a true gopher but a ground squirrel (or quite possibly Joe Clark).

And if you're out of the Rockies and onto the prairies, odds are you're encountering a Richardson's ground squirrel. These are the cute little gaffers that race back and forth across the Trans-Canada Highway in an effort to demonstrate they really do have tiny little brains. Since most Albertans refer to them as gophers (and let's face it, "gopher" is a funnier-sounding word with an unlimited capacity for punning), I will henceforth refer to them as gophers, unless I know them by their first name, in which case I will use their proper Christian names.

There are, according to one survey that I'm making up as I write this, about 600 million gophers in Alberta, or roughly 200 gophers per Albertan—more than enough to go around, with a few spares left over to make someone a nice cozy pair of underwear.

Albertans have had a love/hate relationship with gophers since, well, forever. Early explorers loved them because they made a nice, light snack. But they also hated gophers because early explorers tended to be a little grumpy. (You try early exploring—it isn't as easy as it looks.)

Tourists love them because they are cute, friendly, approachable, and tend not to tear into your flesh the way a grizzly might. But tourists also hate gophers because of the stain they make on their car tires when they inadvertently run over them, or worse yet, because tourists drive off cliffs trying to avoid running over them. Either way, it isn't pretty.

Naturalists love them because that's what naturalists do and also because gophers are easy to identify and study. But, truth be told, some naturalists also hate them because it's difficult to find a full-time job as a naturalist, so they tend to blame the gopher. I'm not sure why.

Biologists speak of the ecological role gophers play: of their importance in the circle of life and how gophers are one of the most important food items for numerous Alberta predators (and maybe for a few Alberta restaurants). But even some biologists hate the gopher, because it's very hard to get research funding for something that small, uncharismatic, and stupid.

Urbanites love gophers because they like all things wild and free. But they also hate gophers, because gophers remind them that, as urbanites, they themselves are not wild and free.

Which brings us to farmers and ranchers. Alberta has a lot of farmers and ranchers, which still comes as a big shock from time to time to folks living in Calgary and Edmonton. As opposed to a love/hate relationship, it's probably more accurate to say that many farmers and ranchers have a hate/really hate relationship with the little rodents. Gophers raid their crops, dig holes that become death traps for horses and cows, and, worst of all, for such small critters, gophers have surprisingly bad breath. Unless you work the land and live among gophers day in and day out the way these folks do, that is a hardship you can't truly begin to appreciate.

Which brings us, in a roundabout way, to the world-famous Torrington Gopher Hole Museum. If there was a first-place prize for Alberta-themed humour or an award for capitalizing on our love/hate relationship with gophers, it should probably go to the folks who created this oddity of a museum and, in the process, put the wee hamlet of Torrington, Alberta (population 192, unless Bob's gone into Calgary shopping), on the international map.

On one beautiful, crisp September morn, we (mostly I) decided that it was the ideal sort of day to visit Torrington in order to check out the museum (because, trust me, there aren't too many other reasons to visit Torrington).

"Couldn't we have instead gone out for a nice dinner and taken in some theatre in Calgary?" my wife asked while we drove toward the town along pastoral Highway 27. What a great sense of humour my wife has.

We pulled into Torrington (about 100 kilometres northeast of Calgary; 30 kilometres off Highway 2) at about two o'clock. To say that the town is small is like saying I'm a good writer—it's just *that* obvious. A tourist brochure had informed us that we would find the museum on the corner of Second Street and Second Avenue, which now seemed like way too much information, given that there appeared to be only about two streets in all of Torrington.

We stopped first at the town entrance, where the official town mascot, a 4-metre-high gopher named Clem-T. GoFur, greeted us. We learned that Clem-T., born 20 June 1991, was the offspring of one Homer GoFur and Trixie Hydrant GoFur. Is that cute, or what?

We followed the directional signs past Tommy's Diner, hanging a left, then right, then left to the museum. There are no four-way stops or traffic lights in Torrington, but there are eleven fire hydrants, all painted to resemble small gophers. It just doesn't get much cuter than this, folks.

The museum is located in a nondescript building about the size of a trailer. A small gift shop awaits visitors in the

Gopher fire hydrants. Does it get cuter than this?

entranceway, where one can purchase assorted gopherish items: gopher calendars, certificates verifying that you have visited the world-famous museum, gopher placemats, and gopher "Do Not Disturb" signs. You can even get a sign saying "We HOLED up for a while in Torrington, Alberta, Canada." Cute. Cute. Cute.

Adult admission to the museum was only two dollars. I pointed out to my wife that was considerably less expensive than a nice dinner and theatre experience in Calgary.

The entire museum takes maybe fifteen minutes, tops, to tour. There are forty-one displays featuring seventy-three stuffed gophers, all dressed as different characters, all in different poses, most portraying scenes from daily life in Torrington (which would likely explain why there was no gopher brothel scene).

A few other visitors were in the museum, and the reaction seemed to be the same from everyone: nervous, tittering laughter backstopped by stunned amazement. It truly was one of the goofiest museums I'd ever stepped foot in. The muted laughter, though, soon gave way to out-and-out guffaws as the museum patrons, ourselves included, studied the dioramas more closely.

There were scenes of cowboy gophers riding covered wagons, eating at Torrington's own Tommy's Diner, playing baseball, farming hay, and even a black-masked bandit gopher pulling a bank heist, complete with a tiny gun clutched in his furry little paw. Many of the dioramas had captions accompanying them. The gopher at Tommy's Diner was saying "Boy, am I stuffed" (cue the snare drum), while the hairstylist gopher at the beauty salon was shouting out "I'm a gopher, not a magician!" as she fought with her gopher client's tangle of hair.

I was hard-pressed to choose a favourite scene, but I think I most enjoyed the one where an environmentalist gopher was fighting with another gopher over the body of a gopher that the other gopher is trying to take to the gopher museum (did you follow that okay?). My wife enjoyed the wedding scene, which featured a lovely couple. The gopher groom donned a black tux and top hat, while the gopher bride wore a lovely white wedding gown, presumably designed by Versace.

There was also a fashion show, curling and hockey scenes, a hotel pool hall, seniors centre, mobile home park, Olympic

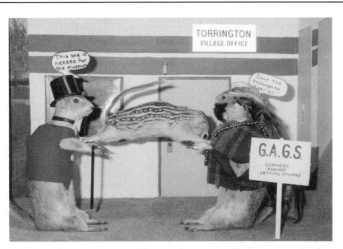

Stuffed gophers parodying their own stuffed gopher display.
Is this deep or what? (Courtesy Torrington Gopher Hole Museum)

medallists showing off their medals (for fastest grain eater, fastest hole digger, and fastest car dodger), even a prehistoric display featuring a little gopher decked out in a primitive fur coat. The church scene included an angel gopher and a gopher fast asleep in one of the back pews, while a romantic moonlit scene offered up a cute little gaffer wearing a teensy weensy black leather jacket. Again, does it get cuter than this? I don't think so.

Most scenes are intended to represent a local area theme. The museum has received requests for other additions, most notably for a little Lady Diana gopher or perhaps a Jean Chrétien gopher. But it doesn't want to go down that road, because likely the road would end up with a fat, drooling Elvis gopher passed out in a drug-induced coma in a dingy bathroom. Nobody wants to see that.

The museum welcomes thousands of visitors from all over the world each summer. Which brings us to perhaps the most fascinating part of the museum—and back to our love/hate theme.

You see, the Gopher Hole Museum has embraced the saying "There's no such thing as bad publicity" with open, furry

Few people realize just how religious Alberta gophers really are. (Courtesy Torrington Gopher Hole Museum)

paws. Free international publicity unexpectedly landed on its doorstep when People for the Ethical Treatment of Animals (PETA) expressed outrage. The Torrington tourism folks replied to PETA's concerns with a postcard that simply read "Get Stuffed." Even Premier Ralph jumped into the controversy by defending the museum in the press, while articles about the offbeat museum were featured in *Newsweek* and the *Wall Street Journal.*

Despite threats to do so, no animal rights groups showed up to protest when the museum opened its doors in 1996. That doesn't mean the museum hasn't got its share of mixed press. In binders and scrapbooks, you'll find clippings of all the international media attention, as well as a spate of pro- and anti-gopher museum letters, which are at least as entertaining as the stuffed gophers themselves, perhaps even more so.

The letters and articles come from as far away as England, Germany, Japan, and Australia. One article was rather curiously titled "An Alien in Weirdville: Accidental Tourist Finds the Essence of Canada in the Gopher Museum." (Wow, the essence of Canada!)

What really stands out is the emotion conveyed in many of the comments:

"You would have to be pretty sick and pretty stupid to think it was okay to do this!"

"Screw PETA we love you!"

"Please let the rats live!"

"Gophers have the right to enjoy the beauty of life, and they have barely begun to live their lives!"

"Why don't you create a stuffed PETA museum instead?"

"The animal activists should go stuff themselves!" (from the mayor of Torrington)

"Congratulations to the mayor for telling the animal rights groups to go stuff themselves!"

"Dear mayor, stuff this!" (including a drawing highlighting a certain finger)

After reading the dozens and dozens of letters and articles, I realized that stuffing gophers and putting them on display is a hot button issue for many folks—and the town of Torrington couldn't be more thrilled. In the first year, more than nine thousand people from as far away as England, Russia, India, and Japan visited the museum. On average, about six thousand visitors come each summer.

So it just goes to show you that when you go fer something a little offbeat, a little con-Torrington-versy can go a hole long way.

Why does Saskatchewan want Alberta to separate from Canada?

Because it will be a closer drive to BC for them.

———————————————

Why does Alberta have daylight savings time, but Saskatchewan doesn't?

Who wants to spend another hour in Saskatchewan?

make a break for the border

L loydminster, Alberta, represents one possible answer to that devastatingly insightful question "Where does Alberta end and Canada begin?" Or should I say, Lloydminster, Saskatchewan? Either answer is possible, since Lloydminster, Alberta/Saskatchewan, is Canada's only city with a schizophrenic personality disorder, courtesy of the fact that it straddles the provincial boundary.

If civil war between Saskatchewan and Alberta ever broke out, Lloydminster would clearly be the battlefront. In fact, I harbour strong suspicions that Saskatchewan is already using Lloydminster as a port of entry into our province, as a base camp for nefarious spy activities, and, most important, as a place where Saskatchewanians can save a few precious pennies on provincial sales tax. I fear that little green people are walking among us in Lloydminster, decked out in their Roughriders sweatshirts, pretending to be *just like us*.

As a pressing issue of provincial security, I felt it was my duty to look into this matter for myself. This is my report.

Lloydminster is named for the Reverend George Exton Lloyd, who, along with Reverend Isaac Montgomery Barr, recruited some two thousand Britons in a quest to form an all-British colony in the wilds of Canada's North-West Territories in 1902. Due to a number of factors (that I don't have time to get into, not with provincial security on the line), Barr was ousted from the colony, while Lloyd was deemed a worthy enough leader to have the new town named in his honour. (The name Lloydminster actually means "Lloyd's monastery," which is likely why people reputedly have a tough time scoring in Lloydminster bars.)

Things got interesting in 1905, when the Feds began divvying up the pie out west. The town just happened to have settled on the future boundary line (the fourth meridian) dividing Saskatchewan and Alberta. The provincial boundary split the town roughly down the middle. The Saskatchewan side became an official town in 1907, while the Alberta side remained a humble village.

But wait! Things get even more interesting! And you can tell things get more interesting because I'm using exclamation marks! In 1930, the two halves amalgamated into one town, ignoring the potential governance pitfalls of being separated by a provincial boundary. The 1930 amalgamation featured a lovely mock wedding ceremony; however there was no word, at least none I could find, on who played the blushing, nervous bride, and if she wore white. In 1958, Lloydminster upgraded its status yet again to become a full-fledged city.

Today, the provincial boundary runs along Fiftieth Avenue. Lloydminster falls under the two provinces' respective municipal acts, but a special charter, which had to be passed by both provinces, authorizes the city to deal with many of its interprovincial border issues itself.

Now let me ask you: Does it get more Canadian than this? Forget about the two solitudes, the whole French and English question—Lloydminster is where the *real* Canada hits the pavement, baby. This is where two completely distinct, unique cultures stand back to back, face to face, and side to side, living not as Albertans or Saskatchewanians, but as Canadians. (Or, quite possibly, Albatchewans, or maybe Saskbertans?)

At least, *some* of the residents are living like this. I still had too many pressing doubts about Lloydminster and knew that only a field trip to the city—located about two and a half hours east of Edmonton along the Yellowhead Highway—would squelch these nagging concerns.

I arrived from the south, via Highway 17, which follows beside the Alberta/Saskatchewan border, the infamous "Straw Wall" itself—North America's longest straight surveyed line (and if *that* doesn't send alarm bells ringing, I don't know what would). Saskatchewan was now just a few feet to the east of me as I cruised the prairie highway. Although I didn't see any suspicious activities per se, I could just feel it in my bones that they were up to something over there.

I saw a boy, maybe twelve years old, out in a field right along the border playing with a yellow lab. But like a crooked painting in an area not prone to getting earthquakes, something didn't seem quite right. The more I thought about him, the more I thought that he wasn't really a boy, and it wasn't really a yellow lab, and they weren't really "playing" at all.

My suspicions escalated when I realized that although I was still in Alberta, every car that passed me had Saskatchewan plates on it. Had an invasion already begun right under our very innocent Albertan eyes? Were farmers, on the pretense of running out for milk, actually conducting recon missions deep into the eastern hinterland of Alberta? And what the hell does their licence plate tagline—"Land of Living Skies"—mean, anyway?

As I pulled into the city of twenty-two thousand, I tuned into the tourist information radio station. The entrance sign welcomed me to "The Border City," while the taped radio message urged me to "make a break for the border," which seemed like a rallying cry right out of the wild, wild west. What sort of lawless society was living up here that would urge innocent people to "make a break for the border"?

Listening to the radio, it became apparent that the city was trying to capitalize on its border-straddling ways. The narrator made mention of the fact that this was "Canada's only border city" about every eight seconds. In fact, if memory serves correct, the radio narration sounded something like this: "Why not make a break for the border at Canada's only border city, Lloydminster, the Border City? The Border City sits right on the border, and as such is Canada's only border city, so why not make a break for the border, here in Canada's only border city? In the Border City, you can make a break for the border because we're Canada's only border city, so make a break now to Canada's border city, sitting, you guessed it, right on the border!"

And on and on it went. Although, owing to my heightened state of alertness (which was revved up to "Level Green," a new security level designed to help people be on the lookout for

Roughriders fans disguised as Stampeders fans), my mind may have been playing tricks on me.

Given that they made such a big deal of the border, I was surprised that it was almost hidden from sight as I drove through town. Driving along the Fourth Meridian/Fiftieth Avenue/Highway 17, I had to strain to see the discreet signs indicating the boundary line's presence. I think if it wants to push this border theme, Lloydminster really needs to consider building a Berlin-style wall separating the two provinces, or even a moat of sorts, filled with gators, or a canal filled with gondoliers.

I soon noticed that people were crossing the border without any sort of security checks or passport clearance. Then I remembered we were still in Canada, and that *technically*, if Saskatchewan people wanted to enter our province without any sort of harassment, they were entitled to do so. Still, it didn't sit well with me.

Interviewing several locals, I discovered that not only did people move freely back and forth across the border, but that some actually had *friends or relatives* on the other side. Moreover, some folks lived in one province, yet worked in the other, or, God forbid, vice versa. It was like these people were living as rats, scurrying back and forth across the invisible line to take advantage of what the other province had to offer.

"Oh, cheap gas in Alberta!" Scurry, scurry, scurry.

"Oh, cheaper houses in Saskatchewan!" Scurry, scurry, scurry.

"Oh, no provincial sales tax in Alberta!" Scurry, scurry, scurry.

"Roughriders are *Canada's* team!" Scurry, scurry, scurry.

"I can drink in Alberta when I'm eighteen!" Scurry, scurry, scurry.

"A higher minimum wage in Saskatchewan!" Scurry, scurry, scurry.

"Oh, is Ralph running again?" Scurry, scurry, scurry. (I'll let you choose the direction of the scurry on this one.)

I also noticed it was hard to distinguish folks, to discern just who was a Saskatchewanian and who was an Albertan. It was like some massive, accelerated Darwinian experiment was underway here, where two previously distinguishable races of people had melded into one super race. And then I recalled the classic 1956 movie *Invasion of the Body Snatchers*, wherein humans couldn't identify who the alien pod people were either. In the movie, just like in Lloydminster, they looked, talked, and acted *just like us.*

I tentatively ventured over to the Saskatchewan side for a visit to the Barr Colony Heritage Cultural Centre. Despite the out-of-province location, I have to admit this is a very impressive museum, housing a fantastic display of art, a tremendously creative oil exhibit, and other assorted historical displays. Still, there was one exhibit called Bunnyland that creeped me out a bit. It featured assorted stuffed bunnies dressed up and participating in human activities, such as playing poker, pushing a baby in a stroller, and playing the accordion. Sure, we've got our Torrington Gopher Hole Museum in Alberta, but come on—*bunnies*? I would have expected something like this from Saskatchewan.

Back into the heart of the city now, I stopped a few more locals and asked them, if they had to choose just one province for Lloydminster, which province would it be, Saskatchewan, Alberta, or Manitoba?

"Well," one long-time resident named Jess told me, "I think most of our hearts are aligned with Saskatchewan, but now, unlike the old days, two-thirds of the folks live on the Alberta side. So I'd have to say . . . Manitoba." Exactly the answer I expected from a subversive Saskatchewanian trying to divert the issue elsewhere.

He was right though, a look at the census figures over the years revealed that the Saskatchewan side outnumbered the Alberta side almost two-to-one until the 1950s, when the Alberta side suddenly began to outpace Saskatchewan at an increasing rate. Now, Albertans outnumber the Saskatchewan folks three to one.

So maybe I was being paranoid? Maybe there is no conspiracy? Maybe I imagined the whole underground grain railways? I mean, people really did seem content there. They were living, working, playing, and even sleeping side by side with one another in Eden-like harmony. Perhaps my initial instinct was right—could this really be what Canada is all about? Is this where we're headed—a country undivided by borders, one seamless nation united only by our love for hockey, beer, and doughnuts? Canadians first, Albertans second?

what's so <u>funny</u> about alberta?

Who am I kidding? Until we truly embrace our love for hockey, beer, doughnuts, *and* the Canada Health Act, poutine, cod cheeks, the Vancouver Canucks, and Red Green, we'll all just have to keep going about our separate ways.

But at least Lloydminster stands as living, breathing proof that there is hope for all of us.

Even in Canada.

"Hello, is this the weatherman?" asks the Edmontonian over the phone one morning in late May.

"Yes, it is," replies the weatherman. "What can I help you with?"

"Well," the man says, "I wanted to let you know that I just finished shovelling two metres of partly sunny off my front porch."

when it's winter in july, how could you not laugh?

I t has been said that an Albertan is someone who is prepared for skiing in August and golfing in February. I know it has been said because I just finished saying it. Maybe it's only me who said it, but there is some truth lurking somewhere behind that comment. After all, Alberta is famous for its wacky weather—so wacky that sometimes all you can do is laugh.

I mean, what else is there to do but laugh when your camping trip in July is postponed due to snow, or when an *absence* of snow plays havoc with the Winter Olympics? Or when winter *follows* spring, as it so often does, followed shortly thereafter by summer, then spring again, winter, spring, winter, spring, then finally summer? Or when hail-stones the size of prairie oysters pummel your cowboy hat? Or when you drive to Edmonton and experience all five seasons in a single trip? (I'm sure Albertans would agree that we deserve to be recognized for having *at least* five seasons.)

In fact, I'd venture to say that it is our unpredictable weather that accounts for Albertans' sense of humour, or lack thereof, depending on how badly the weather has screwed you over.

In light of all the wacky weather Alberta receives, here is what the average Albertan, above-average Albertan, or Albertan tourist needs to know in order to survive happily in our five-season province:

- Always bring snowshoes. Yes, this means that even when heading out to the opera in mid-July, one would be prudent to strap a pair of snowshoes to the back of one's strapless black evening gown.

- If you hear someone yell "Twister!" in the middle of Alberta, chances are they're not talking about the party game.

- Spring lasts an average of two and a half days, so if you have spring cleaning to do, plan accordingly.

- Never try to catch an Alberta hailstone in your mouth.

- Never purchase a ski season pass until you are absolutely certain of snow conditions for the year. This means you should buy your pass sometime around mid-March.

- When visiting Lethbridge, keep your body tilted forward at a twenty-five degree slope at all times or you'll topple over.

- Because of the unpredictable nature of the water supply, try not to take up farming in the southern half of the province. (Oops!)

- Never invite your in-laws to stay with you during a chinook. (Both crime rates and crankiness soar during chinooks.)

- Don't take your snow tires off until . . . until . . . well, ever.

- If you can't afford a trip to Mexico, Medicine Hat is a swell alternative: plenty of sunshine, it still starts with the letter "M," and there's a great little Mexican restaurant in downtown Medicine Hat. (Your spouse will never know the difference, especially if he or she drinks a lot.)

- Always dress in layers between February and July, then again from August through to the end of January. The best approach to layering is to start with a Speedo, top with a pair of Bermuda shorts, then long underwear, then jeans, then snowpants; on top go with a T-shirt, shirt, pullover sweater, light spring jacket, windbreaker, fleece, and down parka.

- Never pursue a career as a meteorologist or a groundhog in Alberta. Edmonton groundhogs are some of the worst of Canada's groundhog prognosticators—correctly forecasting the length of winter only 26 percent of the time.

deep questions posed by tourists in alberta

Is West Edmonton Mall just a parking lot?

Is Edmonton open in the winter? How about Alberta?

How do I get to Dead Deer?

How do I get to Medical Hat?

Are the prices in Alberta restaurants in Canadian money or American money?

Do you have gas stations in Alberta? How about milk?

Do you ticket people in Alberta?

Do you have phones in Alberta?

the mother of all malls

Upon arrival at the Edmonton International Airport, I told the cabbie to ferry me away immediately to that crazy funhouse where the silliness and shopping never stops.

So he drove me posthaste to the Alberta Legislature. A fun guy, my cabbie.

"No, no, my good man," I said, "I meant West Edmonton Mall, or as I like to call it—'WEM.'"

He spirited me off once again, following the directional signs to the mall. The signs, I couldn't help but notice, feature a polka-dotted creature with antennas that looks remarkably like an alien with chicken pox. Is this the WEM mascot—an alien? Perhaps it's a bug of some sort? What the hell is it? Is this what I'll look like after eight hours of intense shopping?

Before long, the monster mall loomed in the distance like a mighty pyramid (only without any of that interesting architecture or historical significance stuff dragging it down).

As we approached the mall, then circled in the WORLD'S LARGEST PARKING LOT (and one wonders why it is that Edmonton has more land per capita than any other North American city?), I suddenly felt as though I was aboard a tiny aircraft awaiting clearance to land. Upon receiving the a-okay from air traffic control, my taxi driver dropped me off at one of the mall's back entrances. Or was it the front? Or the side? It was hard to say really. There are, I am told, fifty-nine entrances in total. So I knew that even after spending years hiking in the rugged wilds of the Canadian Rockies, I didn't have a hope of finding my way back to this same spot again.

Upon entering the mall, I was immediately struck by its

mallness. There were, for example, shops and shoppers, two things one would expect to see in a mall. But this, of course, wasn't just any mall. No, this was WEST EDMONTON MALL (cue the booming echo).

Opened in 1981, WEM is touted as being the largest mall in the known galaxy! (Actually, *I'm* touting the "known galaxy" part. WEM just claims to be the biggest mall in the world. But do you know what would really impress me? The world's smallest mall. Imagine the short lineups and stress-free parking at that little puppy. It would be shopping heaven! But I digress and really should get out of these parentheses before you lose your train of thought.)

So where was I? Oh yes, so the mall is honking big. How big is WEM? It's 48 hectares big, or, as the mall proudly proclaims, the equivalent of 100 football fields or 48 city blocks of mallness, or roughly the same size as about half a dozen rural Alberta towns. (In fact, rumour has it there is a small Alberta town swallowed up somewhere inside the mall.) And the mall is chock full to the rim with more than 800 STORES AND SERVICES, so presumably there are things you'll find in WEM that you didn't even know you needed.

Let's put this size thing in perspective, since it is WEM's claim to fame. WEM is, like the Great Wall of China, clearly visible from space, making it the mall of choice for intergalactic travellers. The mall is so huge that it creates its own weather systems, or so I've been told by a reliable meteorologist.

Not only that, I've been told by some unreliable sources that the mall has its own head of state, flag, national anthem, and a navy that rivals Canada's fleet. In fact, the place is so massive that if I was a ruthless dictator hiding weapons of mass destruction, well . . . let's just say you can rent some pretty hefty retail space at WEM, and leave it at that, shall we?

And chew on this for a moment: The mall has thirteen different postal codes. Thirteen! I've been to Alberta towns that didn't merit half a postal code, and WEM has thirteen! Shoppers can actually mail postcards to their friends at the other end of the mall.

Fortunately, the mall sucks up only the equivalent amount of electricity as a community of about 50,000 people and uses a mere 22.8 million litres of water (roughly half the Pacific Ocean), excluding the aquariums (which presumably don't use water). And to feed the mall its daily intake of shoppers, you of course need THE WORLD'S LARGEST PARKING LOT (boy, there's something to be proud of). It's also home to the largest indoor lake (because who doesn't enjoy getting back to the great indoors for the weekend), the largest indoor amusement park, the largest indoor wave pool, and the tallest indoor permanent bungee jump tower (as opposed to the scores of *temporary* indoor bungee jump towers evidently dotting the landscape). The mall has even been called the Eighth Wonder of the World, presumably by people who don't spend a whole lot of time wondering about things.

So, given the mall's bloated size, where does one begin? Facing more than 800 STORES AND SERVICES and 110 EATING ESTABLISHMENTS, I knew I needed a plan, and my plan was this: stagger dopily forward along with the other shoppers, and no one, especially me, would get hurt.

I should point out that I was fully prepared for my field trip through the mall. In fact, I may have been overprepared—I seemed to be the only person donning a backpack, hiking boots, and climbing helmet. I'd even pre-registered with the search and rescue people, in case, God forbid, something went awry. Because I just hate it when something goes awry.

Fumbling for my compass, I quickly chose to forgo my staggering-dopily-forward plan and boldly struck out in a northeast direction with the intent of conducting a recon mission by circumnavigating WEM. Total time to complete circumnavigation: 1 hour and 47 minutes.

Here is my final recon report:

2:20 PM: Pass by young girl talking excitedly on cell phone explaining to friend that she is learning how to walk in a new pair of $500 shoes. Have sudden urge to buy new shoes. Is shopping contagious, I wonder?

2:22 PM: Already passing by the thirteenth lingerie store and ponder the statistic that more Albertans sleep in the nude than in any other province. (Let me clarify: I don't mean to suggest Albertans sleep nude when in Alberta, but not in the buff when we venture over to Saskatchewan. I'm saying that a higher percentage of Albertans sleep in the nude than do people from Ontario, or any other province.) So if we have such a high percentage of au natural sleepers, who's buying all this lingerie?

2:28 PM: Pass by mini-golf. But since this is WEST EDMONTON MALL, it's not just any mini-golf, it's . . . ADVENTURE GOLF!

2:32 PM: Pass by a replica of the *Santa Maria*. Sign lets people know that the ship is an exact replica and is available for receptions and private functions—just the way Christopher Columbus would have liked it.

2:36 PM: Find book about West Edmonton Mall in bookstore. For only $9.95, you can purchase a book full of promo shots of the very mall you are in. A wave of despair cascades over me.

2:45 PM: Enter the WORLD'S LARGEST INDOOR LAKE AND WAVE POOL (promoted by WEM as a "year-round beach paradise!"). Observe people sitting on plastic chairs reading novels. They seem to be mistaking the WORLD'S LARGEST INDOOR LAKE for Florida or perhaps "a year-round beach paradise." Suddenly wish I was in Florida.

2:47 PM: Get escorted out of wave pool by security guard after being told that wearing a thong is not permitted in the WORLD'S LARGEST INDOOR LAKE.

2:56 PM: Stroll through the mother of all food courts. Look for place to sit down but sculpture of man eating a burger is taking up only available chair. Whose idea was this? Is the statue meant to be instructional, so that we know what the chairs are for?

2:57 PM: Notice that there is not just one, but two McDonald's outlets in close proximity, just in case the first Big Mac doesn't stick, I suppose. Feel further despair for my planet.

3:04 PM: Pass by dolphin exhibit. Signs warn shoppers not to throw coins in the pool because it "endangers the dolphin." No mention of what sticking a dolphin into a mall does to dolphins. Read sign of upcoming show on penguins. Penguins. Edmonton. Alberta. Shopping mall. Made sense to me.

3:05 PM: Consider riding in famous WEM submarine. Consideration thankfully passed. Believe now it was actually a bout of gas.

3:13 PM: Run into legendary Mall Child. Had thought Mall Child, an orphan child raised entirely in the mall, was an urban legend, but here he was. (See "Interview with Mall Child" on pages 133-34.)

3:18 PM: Stroll around skating rink. Nothing funny

about a skating rink. I move on.

3:24 PM: Notice a place to get loans. Could come in handy in a place like this.

3:27 PM: Stroll past second adult store. Nice to know that if you forgot something at the first one, you don't need to backtrack.

3:33 PM: Mail postcard to friend at far end of mall. Postal outlet workers look at me funny.

3:41 PM: Stroll by Hooters Restaurant. First food court I've seen with a Hooters.

3:43 PM: Go to amusement park. Whack moles at Whack-a-Mole game. Kick ass on moles and reclaim title as World's Greatest Mole Whacker, a title I've held off and on since 1976.

3:46 PM: See sign in store saying "Today only, bras half off!" Not caring which half is off, I find that my whole shopping experience suddenly improves.

3:51 PM: As I pass by the 743rd store, am haunted by the thought, "There must be *something* I need?"

3:54 PM: Pass by shoe girl on cell phone again. This time telling another friend about her shoes, only now they cost $600.

4:07 PM: Exhausted, return to starting point.

Total expenditures: 0

Total kilometres logged: 87.5

And that's how I spent my day in the mall. Please don't get defensive about my semi-sarcastic remarks. I do realize that WEM is a major tourist facility that brings gazillions of dollars into Alberta's economy. It's just that I'm a typical male and really don't have the shopping gene. That, and the fact that my mother abandoned me in a mall at a young age, has left me with an unnatural fear of malls, so actually making it in and out of WEM without having a nervous breakdown was quite an accomplishment for me.

interview with mall child

I can guarantee you that Mall Child, although dismissed as an urban legend, really does exist. In fact, I sat down with Mall Child at the West Edmonton Mall food court.

Mall Child was decked out in the latest Gap wear, slurping a large Coke slushie, and sucking back some greasy fries. If not for his frighteningly pale complexion, he could have passed for any of the hundreds of teens drifting aimlessly through the mall.

Me: "So you're the world-famous Mall Child?"

Mall Child: "Yes."

Me: "Do you know how you came to be here?"

Mall Child: "My mother traded me in for a new pair of shoes."

Me: "How does that make you feel?"

Mall Child: "Okay. They were nice shoes."

Me: "How have you managed to survive all this time?"

Mall Child: "Like everyone else. On credit."

Me: "Uh. And is it true you've never been outside?"

Mall Child: "Yeah, that's true. My eyes and skin can't adjust to the natural sunlight."

Me: "Doesn't that make you sad?"

Mall Child: "Like, no, not really. I have everything I could ever need here. A lake, skating rink—"

Me: "Hooters?"

Mall Child: "Yeah, sure, Hooters, fast food restaurants, an amusement park, lots of other kids, doughnuts, video games ..."

Me: "What about school?"

Mall Child: "What could I possibly learn in school that I can't learn here? I mean, this is a microcosm of humanity. It's all here, like, I mean, sooner or later everyone goes shopping, right?"

Me: "Well, I guess so. So do you plan to spend your entire life here?"

Mall Child: "Of course. I'd like to meet a nice Gap girl maybe, settle down, and have some Gap babies, or, I don't know, I guess just hang out and shop and stuff. Anyway, I gotta run, there's a sale—"

Me: "A sale, where?"

Mall Child: "I dunno, somewhere. There's *always* a sale, mister."

And with nary a glance back, Mall Child disappeared into the crowd.

fantasy island

Checking into Edmonton's Fantasyland Hotel, I half expected to see Mr. Roarke and Tattoo standing side by side at the door, dressed smartly in their white tuxedos, Tattoo shouting "De taxi! De taxi!" in that annoyingly endearing scratchy voice of his.

How can you *not* want to stay at a hotel with the word "fantasy" in its name? The Fantasyland Hotel is tucked (in a massive sort of way) into a corner of West Edmonton Mall, making it the destination of choice for Edmonton-bound mall rats and humorists wanting to seek out a little Alberta humour and a good time.

The hotel offers a number of fantasy-related theme rooms, none of which are featured in any of my own fantasies—for example (and curiously enough), they don't have a theme room called Chocolate-Covered Supermodels.

Of course, being a family-oriented hotel, the hotel offers themes somewhat tamer than my tastes, including the Canadian Rail Room, African Room (complete with real lions!), Polynesian Room (featuring a pair of actual Polynesians!), Waterpark Room (complete with hot and cold running water!), Hollywood Room (complete with the Hollywood actor/actress of your choice!), Arabian Room, Roman Room (with your very own gladiator!), Igloo Room (complete with real polar bears!), Victorian Coach Room, Western Room (complete with real cowboys!), and the Truck Room. (I'm kidding about the lions, Polynesians, actors, gladiator, and polar bears.) I'm not really kidding about the cowboys, since I did see some lurking by the ice machine. You can also stay in just a normal executive room, but why on earth would anyone go to the Fantasyland Hotel and choose normal? The only reason I can think of is that they are a highly abnormal person and selecting a normal room would be something far removed from their everyday experience.

As you can guess, I had a bit of a dilemma—which room would I choose for my one wild night of Edmonton-based fantasy? The Igloo Room sounded too cold, especially since it was already minus forty degrees outside. The Roman Room sounded enticing, since I really enjoy wearing togas (and, I might add, look mighty fine in one). And the African Room sounded rather exotic, but my wife was worried about tsetse flies.

My decision turned out to be an easy one to make. Since I was staying at the hotel on behalf of the book, my only recourse was to select the room most reflective of an Albertan theme. It had to be the Truck Room. (Sure, I could have selected the Western Room, but please, don't tell my wife that.)

As I explained to my thoroughly dejected wife, "Alberta is a

The perfect hotel bed for a true-blue Albertan.

truck province. We have more pickup trucks per capita than anywhere else in Canada, so of course we have to stay in the Truck Room!"

Despite my wife's protestations, the Truck Room proved to be the perfect choice—for a little offbeat humour, that is. The walls along the hallway leading to the room were lined with assorted highway signs, while the carpeting featured a yellow-dotted highway line down its centre, making you feel as though you were walking along some sort of surreal highway. (We were even tailgated by someone on the way to the room, which almost led to a nasty incident of hallway road rage.)

The room itself immediately met all my expectations for wackiness. It was everything the aspiring truck owner (or Albertan) could have ever wished for. There were traffic lights, street lights, a bunk bed for the kids in the shape of trucks, an old-fashioned gas pump, a giant stop sign on the wall, and a "Slippery When Wet" sign.

The *pièce de résistance*: an actual yellow truck embedded into the wall! Now when I say "actual yellow truck," that's just what I mean. It was an actual truck! And it was embedded in the wall! And it was bright yellow! And it's where we'd be sleeping! I felt like a ten-year-old all over again as I crawled into my little truck-emblazoned jammies and jumped up and down in eager anticipation of the night ahead.

Until I heard my wife, that is, who was making some sort of derisive comment about the bathroom décor.

"There's a photo of a semi in the washroom," she groused.

"Neato!" I replied.

"Not exactly Martha Stewart design, is it?" she muttered.

"Darn tootin' right, this beats Martha hands down, Little Mama!"

"Little Mama?"

"Yes," I said, "that's the CB handle I'm giving you for tonight."

"And what's yours? 'Trucker Boy'?"

"I was thinking something more macho—like Mongoose."

She disappeared back into the bathroom, leaving me alone in all my truck glory. I climbed the ladder into the back of the pickup truck and flopped onto the mattress. Turning on the fog lights next to the roll bar, I admired the surroundings. Not only was the ceiling above the truck bed mirrored, there was a yellow-dotted highway line running across it, which, I imagined, could help you line yourself up during certain extra-curricular activities.

After hauling my wife into the back of the truck, I snuggled with her against the cab's back window and turned on the television with the remote control.

"See, honey," I said, "you always wanted to go to a drive-in theatre with me. Now you have your chance—this is *exactly* like the drive-in, only without all those annoying people or gigantic screen."

As I surfed channels in pursuit of a *B.J. and the Bear* rerun (because, of course, B.J., if memory serves correct, was a trucker), I said to my wife, "This is very romantic."

She looked at me like I was an alien life form. "Romantic? Wouldn't it be more romantic if you were with someone named Hank?"

I thought about that for a few moments, evidently too many moments, because my wife somehow gained control of the remote, something I would never let happen at home.

After taking the Jacuzzi for a test drive, we ordered some room service: cheeseburgers, fries, and extra gravy, which, I explained to my wife, is something a real truck-kind-of-guy would order.

"Even a truck-kind-of-guy wearing little truck pyjamas?" she replied.

I was a tad disappointed when the burgers arrived courtesy of an ordinary-looking bellhop.

"Disappointed?" my wife asked.

"Yes, I expected him to be dressed up as a tow truck operator," I said glumly.

"Weren't you embarrassed going to the door in your little truck pyjamas?"

"Please quit calling them that," I replied.

After chowing down our burgers, turning off and on the fog lights and traffic lights, we packed it in for the evening. Despite dreaming I was being taken to a monster-truck rally against my will by some guy named Hank, I slept like a baby—a baby tucked into the back of a yellow truck embedded in a wall.

I couldn't wait to get home and redecorate the bedroom.

theme rooms we'd like to see

The King Ralph Room
Comes with a life-sized, realistic mannequin of Ralph overlooking the Jacuzzi and an amazingly accurate Ralph-shaped bed! Plus, for added fun, you can throw anything you want against the walls and nothing ever sticks! On rare occasions, Ralph himself will actually stumble into your room at any and all hours "by mistake."

The Jasper Room
A little overpriced, but sometime during the evening, a bellhop dressed in a bear costume will break into your room and forage through the mini-bar. Includes free T-shirt.

The Banff Room
You and a loved one can recall your glorious early days working in Banff as you sample Kraft Dinner from the mini-bar and share your room and bed with twelve hotel employees. Includes free T-shirt.

The Lethbridge Gone-With-the-Wind Room
Watch the whitecaps in the Jacuzzi as you and a loved one snuggle under the blast of four jumbo jet engines blowing 400-kilometre-per-hour winds over your bed! You'll never experience morning hair like this again!

The Alberta Beef Room
Comes with a mini-bar fully stocked with 100 percent triple Grade A Alberta beef. Relax in the meat-shaped bed while enjoying the room's meat-processing plant décor. Flush the toilet and giggle away to the sound of a mooing cow. And watch out for those meat hooks! After only one night in the Alberta Beef Room, we promise you'll never look at meat the same way again, or your money back!

journey to the centre of alberta

"Hey, I wonder what's over there?"

These immortal words were all that were needed to spark man's ongoing quest to explore his universe. And I say "man" because history has proven that it is mostly men who are stupid enough to explore and stubborn enough not to ask for directions. The twin traits of stupidity and stubbornness, of exploring without asking for

directions, perpetuates a sort of chicken and egg scenario wherein the stubbornness gene ensures that we males have no choice but to keep exploring until we find the right exit out of the suburbs. Alternatively, our lust for exploration feeds a dogged stubbornness that refuses to allow us to stop and ask for directions. It's a vicious cycle.

And I say "stupid enough to explore" because history—and horror movies—informs us that exploring usually results in frostbite, scurvy, starvation, or, especially in the case of horror movies, a hatchet planted firmly into the side of someone's head.

Nonetheless we males are genetically programmed to explore. This is why our sperm swim about in random fashion and why we send out so many at a time—because not one of the little gaffers will bother to stop and ask for directions to the egg. This is why small boys will often attempt to answer the question "What would happen if I tie this rope to my younger brother's torso and attach the other end to our station wagon's trailer hitch?" And this is why grown men, while meandering out and about on summer vacation, always feel a compelling urge to stand on the easternmost point of a province, drive via the highest point of land between Moose Jaw and Sudbury, or have a pee on the westernmost spit of a continent.

I have checked this out with many folks, and they all concur. Women, for the most part, tend not to have the slightest bit of interest in extending a road trip by fourteen hours just to see what the easternmost point of Minnesota looks like, whereas most men would never pass up such an obviously compelling opportunity for exploration. Women will look at a road map and say, "Why don't we take this route? It looks like the straightest line between point A and point B," whereas men are prone to say, "But if we go *this* way, it will take us right around this jut of land that looks remarkably like the shape of a moose's dewlap, and it will add only seventeen hours to the entire trip! And why would we miss out on the chance to drive around something that looks like a moose's dewlap?"

Part of this inner desire to explore likely has something to with our competitive nature. When a man proudly informs his fellow dinner guests that he has just scaled the highest peak in Alberta, some other male is always ready to chime in with, "Hmmm, interesting. But have you ever stood on the easternmost point of land in Minnesota?"

All of this is by way of saying that when I found out that it was actually possible to stand in the *exact* geographic centre of Alberta, I just knew I had to go there. The internal explorer inside me started saying things like "Wow, I could stand right in the centre of Alberta! Not just *close* to the centre, but the actual centre! And then I could tell people that I stood in the centre of the province. And then they'd say, 'Wow, the very centre?' And I'd say, 'Yes, the very centre.' And then we'd all agree that was a neat thing to do. Especially the males." That's what my inner explorer—my mini-voyageur, if you will—was saying.

"Will there be food in the centre of Alberta?" my wife asked. "Would you like me to pack you a sandwich?"

I declined the offer for food and bravely struck out on my journey to the centre, knowing full well that the scenery would be less than overwhelming, that the journey might be a little dull, and that the entire experience could be rather uninspiring. All those considerations were, of course, somewhat insignificant when contrasted against the weighty knowledge that I would be able to stand in the very centre of the province. You can only imagine my giddy excitement.

?

A speaking engagement had brought me to Lac La Biche, conveniently and predictably located on the shore of Lac La Biche, a couple of hours northeast of Edmonton. This provided me with the golden opportunity to accomplish my mission, as the geographical centre would now be only some four or five hours out of my way on the return trip home. This, for a true explorer, is the equivalent of reaching for a beer bottle on the far side of a coffee table.

The morning after my talk, I left Lac La Biche at the crack of dawn, or at least within several hours of the crack of dawn, which made it seem much more like the gaping canyon of dawn. It was a glorious June day, the perfect sort of day to do a little navel gazing.

My journey to the centre of the province led me west out of Lac La Biche along Highway 55, through the tiny town of Grassland, where there were no grasslands, at least not in the grassy sense, but there *was* a goofy-looking statue of a man made out of tires on the west side of town, so all was not lost. The statue looked like some sort of bizarre homage to the gods, but I couldn't for the life of me remember which god represented tires.

Half an hour later, after spilling coffee all over myself in Athabasca, I vowed never to return there, or at least to stop drinking coffee, but I knew it was only the coffee speaking. Especially the coffee that had landed on my crotch.

From Athabasca, my route took me south along Highway 2, then west along Highway 18 through Westlock—"The Best Bloomin' Town in the West." It really was a bloomin' pretty town, complete with a beautiful red brick church just off the main drag.

As I made my way to the centre, I noticed that the amount of highway construction got worse and worse, leading me to believe that perhaps the centre of the province may be some sort of constructional black hole, sucking in highway crews from the farthest reaches of Alberta. There were delays and flag persons so numerous that it gave me the perfect chance to test a theory I have about flag people—that they wouldn't like it much if you ignored their stop sign. (And, boy, I tell you, give someone a little stop sign and an orange jumpsuit and suddenly they think they're the freakin' emperor of the freakin' highway.)

Having waved goodbye to the last flag person, I turned northwest onto Highway 33 and headed toward Swan Hills along the exciting-sounding Grizzly Trail. I didn't see any grizzlies, but I did pass a forlorn-looking moose (have you seen any other kind?) and several herds of bison, presumably captive.

The traffic was remarkably light, making me wonder if I was indeed approaching the centre. After all, wouldn't there be thousands of patriotic Albertans flocking to the centre of the province on such a strikingly beautiful June day?

Not only were there *not* thousands of people, there was scarcely a sign indicating the pull-off to the centre of Alberta parking lot. In fact, if you were paying attention to the highway or other motorists, you would have missed the sign welcoming travellers to "Discover the Centre of Alberta!" altogether. Fortunately, I was not paying attention to the highway, so I found the parking lot some 26 kilometres west of the settlement of Fort Assiniboine.

As I pulled into the deserted lot on the highway's north side, the centre of Alberta suddenly felt like a very lonely place. I got out and surveyed my surroundings. The area was rather flat, which made sense. Wandering over to the trailhead kiosk (thankfully one can't drive to the centre, or I'm certain the joint would have been overrun by explorative wayward dads), I was pleased to see a notice about an upcoming organized hike to the centre. (It's important, I felt, that someone was watching out for our centre.) I also thought how fortuitous it was that the exact centre spot was in the middle of a natural area and hadn't turned out to be in some farmer's bathroom.

After studying the trail map, which let me know the hike to the centre was a mere 3 kilometres, I wandered into the aspen forest and sloshed my way along a soggy and buggy path, only to guess half an hour later that I had strolled down the wrong trail. (Don't ask me *how* I guessed, suffice it to say that we explorers can sense when we're hopelessly lost.) Backtracking, I reviewed the trailhead map again and this time took what I hoped was the correct route into the forest. (You'd think if you had been welcomed to "Discover the Centre of the Province!" someone would put up some, oh, I don't know, proper signs?)

Back into the boreal forest, I trundled along a wide trail until a small sign indicated I should hang a left onto a smaller path. So I hung left. And then after a right, then left, then left, then right, then left after a right, then right after a left, then right after a right, and walking through a rather *Blair Witch*–like dense, gnarly spruce forest, I began to think someone didn't want me, or anyone for that matter, to discover the centre of the province after all.

Perhaps it was a grand hoax of sorts? Maybe there was no actual centre? Perhaps, like the magnetic north pole, the centre shifts about the province from time to time? Maybe the centre *was* some sort of black hole where tourists disappeared or where certain people from Saskatchewan ended up? Despite these disturbing thoughts, I sojourned on, as any stubborn and stupid explorer would.

There were no other people on the trail, but there were lots of bugs, which always makes an outing that much more special. There were also numerous songbirds singing about how wonderful life in Alberta is in the springtime, plus a healthy assortment of animal droppings along the path, including coyote, moose, deer, and even bear scat.

The centre of Alberta, it seemed, was quite a hopping place—at least for pooping critters. The bear poop was particularly large and steaming fresh, like a piping hot plate of hash browns, making me consider how sad it would be to be mauled by a bear in the centre of the province. Sure, being mauled anywhere wouldn't be the best of times, but being mauled in the geographic centre of Alberta would, to my way of thinking, really be the pits.

Being a true explorer, and having no one to ask directions of, I continued to meander about the forest. Eventually, it all worked out as it should have: about an hour after leaving the parking lot, after getting lost three or four times, after sinking up to my armpits in a mud hole, I stumbled upon the X—the exact geographic centre of Alberta. Cue the trumpets.

I'm not sure what I expected—an Albertan epiphany of sorts? Violin music? Buried treasure? An ice cream stand? A souvenir shop selling tacky T-shirts saying "I Stood in the Centre of Alberta and All I Got Are These Lousy Mosquito Bites"?

There was something in the centre, though. A statue of a happy grizzly bear sitting atop a high stone pedestal, all surrounded by a white picket fence. The fence gave the whole thing the appearance of a rather odd cemetery. A plaque in the shape of the province (or Bart Simpson's head) on the pedestal below the bear greets new arrivals to the centre with the rather uninspiring message: "Grizzly Trail Promotional Association. Centre of Alberta. L.S. 14-33-63-7-W5. Honorary chairman Ken Kowalski MLA. Surveyed by Ron Chimiuk, July 1989."

Personally, I think the plaque should have read "Welcome, schmuck. You have just managed to stagger your way through this bug-infested forest to the exact geographical centre of Alberta just because it was here. Satisfied?"

Even though the site was along the Grizzly Trail, I was still a tad surprised to find a grizzly representing our navel. After all, for Alberta's centrepiece, I would have expected maybe a gopher or cow or, given the nature of the trail, perhaps even a giant mosquito.

There were picnic tables in the centre, obviously meant to be decorative, since no one in their right mind would sit still in this orgy of bugs for very long. And there was a guest book. The trail register was signed by, as expected, mostly other males stupid and stubborn enough to venture here. Most of the comments complained about the mud or the mosquitoes or the misleading signs, but in a cheery sort of way, the way Albertans are prone to complain, as though we're always more than happy to play the role of Canada's designated martyr. The general tone of the comments can be summed up as follows: "What a great day and glorious hike! Lots of mud, tons of bugs, and the directional signs really sucked. Otherwise, it was just awesome and I was happy to explore this area on behalf of Albertans and Canadians everywhere!"

As any great explorer would, I needed to document my arrival at the centre by photographing the spot. But, to my abject horror, I realized I'd left my camera in the car. What to do? I could wait until some other hikers arrived, in the hope they'd have a camera, but given the mosquito situation, this seemed like an idiotic idea, even for a real explorer. Instead, I simply stood at the spot for a moment to suck up the significance of it all.

Here is what I sucked up: "I'm now standing exactly halfway between Saskatchewan and BC, halfway between the Northwest Territories and Montana. Wow. Imagine that. Pretty neat, eh? God, there are a lot of bugs here." End of sucking up.

Hoping to now share the emotional experience, I pulled out my cell phone and tried calling someone. Alas, there was no cell phone service in the centre of the province. How could this be?

It's probably just as well, since the conversation likely would have gone like this:

Me: "Hey, I'm calling from the Centre of Alberta!"

Friend: "You're in Red Deer?"

Me: "No, the exact centre!"

Friend: "Edmonton? Are you at West Edmonton Mall? Can you buy me something?"

Me: "No, the exact midway point north and south and east and west. The centre!"

Friend: "I already said Red Deer."

And then I'd get annoyed and hang up on the geographically challenged person (whose name, incidentally, is Dave), so it was probably for the best.

After inadvertently swallowing a bug, I knew it was time to leave. I somehow found my way back to the lot, passing no one along the way, stopping momentarily to take a photo of the roadside sign as proof I was at least close to the centre.

Having come this far, I opted for a circuitous route back home to Canmore, through Swan Hills. Upon entering "Alberta's Outdoor Playground," I recalled Ralph Klein's famous comment about how the Swan Hills Hazardous Waste Plant was a popular tourist facility. I considered taking a tour, because the way Ralph had put it, it sounded sort of fun. I imagined there would be fun activities such as "Stick your hand in this jar and guess what it is!" or "Take a whiff of this!" or maybe hunting for glow-in-the-dark frogs. But time was pressing, and this explorer needed to be home by dark.

I did stop at Swan Hills' famous roadside statue depicting a

The sign assumes you won't get lost. How silly of the sign.

swan protecting her young ones from a marauding grizzly bear. (Nature is aggressive up here in Swan Hills—perhaps it's all that hazardous waste?) The statue was impressive. Created by an Edmonton artist using a rare technique, it incorporates 20,000 pieces of steel. Weighing in at an impressive 907 kilograms, the statue has been voted one of the top fifty roadside attractions in Canada. (I bet whoever voted hasn't seen the giant Mundare sausage.)

On through Whitecourt, "The Snowmobile Capital of Alberta," where plans are afoot to build the world's largest snowmobile in hopes of attracting more people like me to the area. There was no snow on the ground, so a visit to the snowmobile capital seemed a little silly. No offence, Whitecourters. Build your giant snowmobile and I'll come back.

At the town of Sangudo, which sounds like a Mexican drink, I pulled in to see its grain elevator/sundial, and maybe get a Mexican drink. The elevator/sundial sits just off Highway 43. It's a sundial in the shape of a grain elevator. Boulders, marking the presence of the sun's shadows, encircle the elevator. Using the sundial, I was able to estimate that it was sometime between 8:00 AM and midnight.

I ventured farther into the tiny town and was somewhat frightened to see a sign saying "Citizens on Patrol." I imagined a posse of Sangudo villagers armed with torches and pitchforks prepared to chase me out of town at the slightest indiscretion.

Carrying on home, I drove a scenic country route that led me past the tranquil and beautiful lakeside resort community of Mulhurst Bay, southwest of Edmonton, where I spied a pink combine parked in front of a country restaurant. A pink combine in Alberta—someone was very brave.

Two prairie thunderstorms, a cheeseburger, two coyotes, four deer, and I was home by nightfall.

"Was it worth it?" my wife asked. "Was it worth it going so far out of your way?"

I gave her my best incredulous look, a look I have practised in the mirror for many years. "Worth it!" I exclaimed in exasperation. "Honey, I stood in the very centre of the province!"

I couldn't wait to tell my fellow explorers. Especially the male ones.

things you really ought to know about alberta

An Expedia.ca survey found that 44 percent of men from Alberta are willing to don a Speedo while visiting a hot country; while 40 percent of Albertan women would join other topless sunbathers when topless sunbathing was the norm.

––––––––––––

Albertans are more likely to sleep in the nude than any one else in Canada. According to a national survey on sleeping habits, 68.1 percent of Albertans sometimes sleep in the buff.

––––––––––––

Calgary is second only to Winnipeg, worldwide, for the consumption of 7-11 Slurpees.

––––––––––––

The first gasoline tax in the country was here in high-gas, low-tax Alberta! Moreover, Alberta was once tax crazy, applying taxes on horsewhips, buggies, even movie tickets!

––––––––––––

According to a poll conducted by Ipsos-Reid, Alberta ranks number one in Canada when it comes to photocopy machine rage—51 percent of Albertans have physically assaulted a photocopier.

way downtown in cowtown

Poor, overworked, overstressed Calgary has had a rough go of it of late. First there was a national survey suggesting that Calgary was not (gasp!) among the most fun cities in the country.

Then, a Calgary resident nominated Calgary as "Canada's Crap Town" in a *National Post* poll, backed up by the following description of Calgary: "Not so much a city, as a lunatic asylum with traffic lights."

And *then*, the City of Calgary passes a "SUPER bylaw," designed, some residents felt, to suck out the last remaining vestiges of fun. The anti-noise bylaw, for example, would reduce the acceptable nighttime noise level to fifty decibels, or, as one paper pointed out, roughly the same level of noise a refrigerator makes, prompting some to dub Calgary the "City that Fun Forgot."

Finally, the cake-topper—a Calgary alderman created an uproar when he publicly suggested there was nothing to do in Calgary.

Nothing to do in Calgary? No fun to be had in Cowtown? The city that fun forgot???

Sadly, it is once again up to me to set the record straight.

My search for Calgary's underbelly of fun and good times began bright and early, because, according to my neighbour's very noisy truck, that's when the fun really begins.

Approaching Calgary, as the foothills gave way to flattened

gophers, I grew increasingly upset about the fun-sucking accusations being tossed Calgary's way. How could a city nicknamed Cowtown *not* be fun? How could a place that finished second in the world in 7-11's Slurpee consumption *not* be a great place to spend a day? This, after all, is a city that attracted 55,000 scantily clad fans to the Red Mile during the 2004 Flames playoff run. A city that has a "Whoa!" traffic sign in place of a stop sign near Spruce Meadows. Now, really, does it get more fun than *that*?

Since we'd need a lot of energy to get us through the day, and since we'd be spending the day in Canada's highest big city (elevationally speaking), we knew where our first stop had to be: the Oraoxygen Spa at the Calgary International Airport. This was the world's first airport oxygen spa, a place where we could suck up some much-needed oxygen to help us get through the day ahead. (Remember the good old days, when water just came from the tap and oxygen came from the air?)

After getting our fill of freshly squeezed oxygen, we decided to joke around with some airport security people. (This, I should probably clarify, is not the best way to find fun in Calgary.) We then spent some charming moments with "Picascow," a fibreglass cow "artist" standing on its hind legs painting a mural of the city skyline on a wall outside the airport. The cow is part of the Udderly Art Cow auction held in 2000, which featured 117 fibreglass cows scattered throughout the city in search of a permanent home, all decorated by local artists. It was an udder success, and just one of many examples that prove, beyond a doubt, that Calgary rocks when it comes to cow art.

Before leaving the airport, we overheard (okay, eavesdropped on) an American talking into a pay phone that evidently wasn't working properly. The poor fellow was speaking at such a volume that the entire departures level could hear him. With great amusement, the gentleman described Calgary's beloved Plus 15 closed walkways as "gerbil mazes" and urged his phone companion to visit Calgary just "for the sake of seeing the giant rat tubes." His call provided the inspiration for stop number two. It was off to the rat race.

The Plus 15 walkways—featuring fifty-seven enclosed pedestrian bridges, spanning some 16 kilometres approximately 4.5 metres (15 feet, hence the name) above street

151

level—are a distinctly Calgary feature, and often overlooked for their ability to provide countless hours of entertainment. Walking tours, overnight backpack excursions, birdwatching, rollerblading, skateboarding, motorcycle racing, and more await the keen Plus 15 enthusiast. Since we were fully loaded up on fresh oxygen, the lack of fresh air was nary a concern as my wife and I navigated the mazes with the tenacity of cheese-deprived mice.

I should note that the Plus 15 walkways are so much fun they even inspired an award-winning movie called *Waydowntown*. The 2000 movie, written and directed by Calgarian Gary Burns, follows four twenty-something professional urbanites who have wagered a month's salary to see who can stay indoors the longest, a feat only a real Calgarian could pull off.

After working up an appetite in the Plus 15s, we realized we hadn't had breakfast yet, so we made our way immediately to the Westin Hotel. Back in 1969, the hotel's bar manager, Walter Chell, invented the Caesar in honour of the opening of a new restaurant.

"Isn't it too early for a Caesar?" my wife asked.

"But it comes with celery," I explained. "Besides, we're not stopping at just a Caesar." (My wife, I must confess, is a bit of a neophyte when it comes to having fun in Calgary.)

No sir, the Caesar was merely the appetizer. Our next stop, where we'd really fill up for breakfast, was none other than the recently opened Krispy Kreme doughnuts.

Now how could anyone say there's nothing to do in Calgary, when all one has to do is consider the fact that brothers Brett and Jared Taylor lined up for a day and a half awaiting the Krispy Kreme grand opening? Clearly, these imaginative, highly motivated young people are a prime example of how, if you just put a little thought into something, the opportunities awaiting the bored Calgarian are endless.

Upon entering Krispy Kreme, we learned from a sign that each store produces, on average, three thousand doughnuts per hour—or twice the number of doughnuts per year you would need to encircle Earth. Which got me thinking, "Why would anyone need to encircle Earth with doughnuts?"

Before we had even queued up to the display counter, a woman handed us a free doughnut each, fresh off the rack.

They were trying to get us hooked before we'd even seen a doughnut! It was tantamount to giving alcohol to someone who had just stopped drinking. Given that I began to lick the display glass and foam at the mouth like a rabid raccoon, I knew they had me hooked. Fortunately, my wife got me out of there before I started going into convulsions.

Next stop—the site of Calgary's proudest moment, Canada Olympic Park. Here, you can stroll the grounds, visit the museum, or take part in the often overlooked Olympic sport of mini-golf.

How many Calgarians does it take to change a light bulb?

Ten. One to change the bulb, nine to talk about how great the 1988 Winter Olympics were.

At the visitor centre, we tested our knowledge at the trivia quiz:

Question 1: What was the first winter sport to be competed at the Olympics?

"I'm going with ice fishing," I confidently told my wife.

Wrong. It was actually figure skating, and get this, it premiered at the *summer* Olympics in 1908. Boy, were they a tad confused about figure skating. Probably Americans.

Question 2: Which sport do you ride headfirst down an ice track?

"I'm going with ice fishing," I confidently told my wife.

Wrong again. Turns out the correct answer is the skeleton (luge being the one where you go feet first).

Question 3: Which sport was only demonstrated once?

"I'm going with ice fishing," I less than confidently told my wife.

Sadly, I again was wrong. Turns out in 1932 they featured dog sledding as a demonstration sport. And, imagine this, ice

153

fishing has never been included as a sport. No wonder we aren't bringing home more gold medals!

Strolling about the centre, we learned lots of fun facts, such as not only did Jamaica enter a bobsled team in 1988, so did the US Virgin Islands and Monaco. Isn't that as fruitless as the United States entering a hockey team?

We also learned about Olympic mascots. During the 1988 Calgary Olympics, some grumpy Albertans complained about Calgary's Heidi and Howdy, a pair of cherubic-looking polar bears. I'm not sure if these folks complained because they didn't know what the mascots were supposed to be, or because they thought they were just a little too cute, or because they were goosed by Heidi. But in Munich, back in '72, they had Waldi the dachshund as their mascot. *Please.*

According to the display, Heidi and Howdy had very strict rules of protocol to follow: "They must not talk, and they must make *as much physical contact* with people as possible [is it just me, or does that sound a little creepy?], try not to run over small children [I have found this is pretty much a great way to live your life in general] . . . and they must be prepared to try out any sport." As proud Calgarians are apt to boast about to this day, not only did Heidi and Howdy try their paws at horseback riding, curling, and skating, they actually took home the bronze as part of the Canadian bobsledding team.

There was also a "special clause" written into the mascots' rules: they were instructed not to hug Mayor Ralph Klein, Olympic Organizing Committee chairman Frank King, or anyone in a dark suit. (Again, this is just one of those common-sense rules I have tried to live my life by.)

Next up we headed for the Ice House—the only totally refrigerated building in the world. I was hoping to see some penguins, but alas had to settle for the next best thing—bobsled, luge, and skeleton athletes practising their stops and starts on an indoor ice track.

"It's cold in here," my wife complained after only a minute.

"It's called an 'Ice House' for a reason, honey," I, so helpfully, pointed out.

Even though the place smelled like stale ice cream, it was a lot of fun watching the athletes make like otters and slide back and forth along the track. In fact, I'm thinking of building an ice house in my basement. In the meantime, I'm definitely planning a trip back to the Ice House—members of the public can sign up to try their hand at these sports, and I'm pretty sure sliding face down on a patch of ice is something I could master, having already done it by accident on numerous occasions.

"Don't you think it's odd that grown men put on skin-tight suits and lie on top of each other?" my wife asked me.

"If they're doing it as athletes in pursuit of an Olympic medal, then no. If they're doing it on weekends just for something different to do, then yes," I replied.

A display in the Ice House caught my eye—it featured four sausage-like bobsledders from the German bobsledding team in Oslo 1952. This team of porkers, weighing in at a total of 472.42 kilograms, won the gold medal that year, prompting officials to limit the maximum team weight to 362.87 kilograms.

There was much more to see at Canada Olympic Park, but sadly we had to leave. There was still too much fun awaiting us. Not to mention a few testicles.

Yes, you read right, I said testicles. We headed straight for Buzzard's, one of Calgary's most authentically western restaurants and the only place in the world you can drink Buzzard's Breath beer and, more importantly, partake in its annual Testicle Festival. The festival of testicles features an array of prairie oysters—a true Albertan delicacy—with such delightful names as Lick, Bite, and Shoot. Participants have to lick some salt, bite into the testicle (how often do you hear that phrase?), then take a shot of tequila. The festival attracts bull testicle–chompers from far and wide.

"How does it taste?" my wife asked as I tentatively chomped down on my first testicle.

"Sort of like chicken," I said, concentrating on hockey stats the entire time I chewed.

Next stop on the Find Fun or Die tour was the world-famous Calgary Zoo, where we played a rousing game at the gorilla exhibit I like to call Spot the In-laws. Later, we said hello to a historical landmark: 10-metre-tall Dinny, a brontosaurus statue built in 1938. Dinny, rumour has it, has some strange things included inside his stomach, such as tires, old car parts, and Jimmy Hoffa.

the winning entry: an albertan rainstorm

The winning entry in the CBC *Alberta Laughs* contest, as determined by a random draw, was the following true story submitted by Linda Henrickson:

A few years ago my friend Maureen and I decided to take an afternoon drive to Okotoks. On the drive home, we rolled down all the windows in my '66 Impala, letting the warm summer air blow through the car. We arrived back in Calgary and pulled up to a red light at a very busy intersection. All of a sudden, it started to rain––there was, in fact, a huge amount of water coming down on my car. It was as if a fire hydrant had been opened and aimed directly at my old Impala. But then, in a split second, I realized the water was only falling on us, making me wonder just what the heck was going on? It was then I realized that we were trapped alongside a double-decker cattle liner, and that a cow on the upper deck was having a really, really good pee. We rolled up our windows as fast as we could and sat looking at each other with looks of utter disgust on our faces. I looked over at the cattle truck and saw the driver laughing as hard as anyone could possibly laugh.

Only in Alberta.

On our way to the University of Calgary, near the giant King Kong scaling the Movie Poster shop on 16th Avenue, we spotted the Yodeling Sausage trailer being towed ahead of us, advertising "The Best of the Wurst." A yodeling sausage trailer and King Kong together at once! Will the fun *ever* stop?

At the University of Calgary, we headed straight for the Social Sciences tower stairwell, where, legend has it, a dramatic tale about Leon the Frog awaits. Sure enough, the legend of Leon was alive and hopping up the staircase.

The story, written in crude black lettering on the concrete stairs all the way up to the thirteenth floor, tells a twisted tale of pumpernickel sandwiches, Arts and Science majors, dissection, Hells Angels, and green wallpaper—it probably makes more sense if you're heavily drugged or have recently dropped something heavy on your head. But I for one say, "If it gets our young people reading *and* exercising, this can only be a good thing."

Our last stop took us to Glenmore Park. According to a Web site I stumbled upon (so it must be true), there's a little-known nude beach in the park. My wife, being on the shy side, stayed in the car. I, on the other hand, boldly stripped down to what Mother Nature—in an obviously cranky mood at the time—gave me.

Strolling the trails, I soon became aware that something was amiss. I mean, I'm an observant guy—the fact that everyone else was wearing clothes sort of stood out. As did the Girl Guide troupe blowing their whistles and screaming at me like I was some sort of freak.

Hightailing it back to the car, I managed to regroup and, more importantly, get dressed. Only later would I learn, through an article in the *Calgary Herald*, that the presence of a nudist beach here has been a long-standing misconception, one that has circulated in a dozen different Web pages.

Given that Glenmore Park is a bit of a mud swamp, infested for much of the year by leeches, ticks, flies, and mosquitoes, I was pleasantly relieved that it was not a clothing-optional site. Besides, Calgary offers more than enough fun without having to get publicly naked. Thank goodness for small miracles.

Finally, our day had come to an end. Sadly, we hadn't even been arrested. Nor did we have time to whack moles at Calaway Park, down ice cream at Heritage Park, toilet paper the Saddledome, moon motorists from the Calgary Tower, or cruise the Red Mile in search of some lingering Flames fever.

But we did, I dare say, achieve our mission. We proved there are more fun things to do in Calgary than there are in, say, Balzac. Of course, now that I've said that about Balzac, I'm going to have to spend a day there too. Is my job *ever* going to be finished?

?

How could a city that has fake horse races be considered dull? Calgary's St. Louis Hotel holds weekly "World Famous Indoor Horse Races," featuring absolutely no horses. Yes, every Friday an announcer ad-libs an entire fake race, complete with racing forms and sound effects of running horses. Bar patrons informally bet on the entirely made-up race. Whoever said you needed horses for a horse race has obviously never been to Calgary.

giddy up, it's stampede time!

"I'm a hurtin' Albertan."
—a post-Stampede refrain uttered by partied-out Calgarians

Once a year Calgary returns to its western roots by holding the Calgary Stampede—"The Greatest Outdoor Show on Earth."

This is the time of year when Calgarians can warmly embrace their inner redneck. When corporate stiffs turn into cowboy wannabes. When everyone, young and old, men and women alike, has a chance to look like Myron Thompson.

Yes, for two weeks in early July, Calgary, in a concerted effort to make up for the rest of the year, actually becomes really fun (just kidding, Calgary, you know I love you crazy nuts), and where anything and everything is possible. Such as people being lassoed at the Calgary Airport as a friendly way of saying "Howdy, visitor, how does it feel to be roped and hogtied like a squealing pig?" Horses being ridden up the stairs of the Calgary Tower. Staged gunfights at Olympic Plaza. "Yahoo!" signs too numerous to count. Hat-stomping contests where masses of people act like crazed animals and destroy cowboy hats by jumping and chewing on them (all in order to win a free hat, which you'll need because you just, you know, destroyed yours). Enough chili cook-offs to launch a space shuttle into orbit. And 8,748 free pancake breakfasts (that's just on the first morning), because nothing makes people happier than free food (especially homeless people, but we won't get into that right now, because I don't think pancake breakfasts are meant for them).

> Stampede pancake breakfasts use up more than 5 tonnes of pancake batter, 2 tonnes of sausage and bacon, and 5,000 bottles of syrup.

In recent years, a small posse of Calgarians has become a little embarrassed by the Stampede. I'm not talking about the animal rights groups who show up in force to protest the eating of corndogs. No, I'm talking about those snobbish, *homo uptightus* Calgarians who feel that a celebration involving hogs and asses is not very becoming for a New Age city with places to go and people to meet. These folks would prefer Calgary—"The Heart of the New West"—be seen as modern, progressive, and a place where hogs and asses would never be caught dead.

Me, I'm with philosopher John Ralston Saul on this one. I also believe that Calgary needs to continue celebrating its unique western heritage. After all, if Calgary doesn't do it, who will? Furthermore, if we stopped holding the Stampede, how could we continue to laugh at people like John Ralston Saul wearing a cowboy hat? Because, and let's be honest here, there are thousands of people, many of them politicians, who should not be seen in public wearing cowboy hats. I'm still having nightmares after seeing Joe Clark and John Manley in cowboy hats several years ago.

> The first Stampede, held in 1912, was meant to be the last Stampede. It was organized, in part, as a farewell to a rapidly disappearing way of life.

So I for one was eagerly anticipating the 2004 Stampede festivities. And I wasn't the only one. Some cowboys from

Bandera, Texas ("Cowboy Capital of the World"), made a 4,000-kilometre trek to the Stampede via horseback. Dubbed the Preparation-H Ride, these dedicated (or severely bored) cowboys rode for 171 days through snow and rain and, well, heck, probably twisters and grizzly bear attacks, to make it to the Stampede. (Okay, okay, the real name of the ride was the Eye Reckon Freedom Ride, in honour of organizer James "Hoot" Gibson's horse, Eye Reckon.)

The University of Calgary was also excited about the Stampede—offering a Stampede 101 university-level course called the Culture of the Calgary Stampede, presumably in an effort to understand three important phenomena:

1. What the hell is a corndog?
2. Who actually eats corndogs?
3. What happens to people after they eat one?

Approximately 1,844,286 mini-doughnuts and 125,000 hotdogs are consumed each year at the Stampede.

Stampede fever was so fervent in 2004 that a famously cranky 816-kilogram bull named Outlaw (since passed away) from Minburn, Alberta, became the first animal ever to ring the opening bell of the New York Stock Exchange. No, they didn't take Outlaw to the Big Apple, they simply strapped a bell to him (wouldn't that be a delightful task?), then launched him out of a gate at the Stampede grounds, while folks from New York watched the bell ringing live, via satellite. The event was a huge success because, as everyone knows, investors love a bull market.

When Stampede stampeded into Alberta this year, I was ready and rarin' to cowboy up (for you city slickers in the crowd, that's a slang term meaning "to be real tough, like a cowboy") for another year of tonsil-straining yahooing.

The first step to cowboying up is to dress appropriately, lest one be humiliated and mistaken for someone from Toronto, which no one wants. The official Stampede wardrobe for men is this: crisp blue jeans (should be blue and made out of jeans), a western shirt (I chose as western as I could get by donning a bright red Hawaiian shirt), a western belt buckle (roughly the size of a loaf of bread, with enough steel to deflect a bazooka attack), a bolo tie (bolo is Spanish for "noose"), bandana (may substitute a pair of old underwear if actual bandana is unavailable), a cowboy hat (preferably one that fits; however, judging from most people attending the Stampede, this is by no means an absolute requirement), and finally, cowboy boots. You know you've got the right fit in a pair of cowboy boots if it feels like your feet are being slowly swallowed by an anaconda.

As for the women's attire, it's well, pretty much the same, I guess. (Truth is, I was too stressed dressing myself and didn't really pay attention to what the womenfolk were wearing.)

Properly attired, my wife and I set out to take on the Stampede, stopping first at the official Calgary Stampede Web site to get our Web-generated cowboy nicknames. The results: I was Michael "Giddie Up 'der Pardner" Kerr, which seemed like a bit of a mouthful, while my wife was Claudine "Two Nose" Dumais. I was a tad disappointed. My wife's name made her sound like someone who could kick some ass. Mine made me sound like a children's entertainer at a horrible cowboy-themed party for spoiled brats.

But, making like a real cowboy, I shook it off, cowboyed up, and rode off to the greatest outdoor show on Earth. Or at least, the greatest outdoor show in southern Calgary.

After parking the car on someone's back porch, thus saving a dollar in parking and a block of walking, we bravely merged into the masses of people flooding the front gates of the Stampede grounds. Upon entering, the first thing that greets you is a bank machine. Instantly, both my sphincter and wallet tightened up a bit.

We moseyed on over to the information booth, causing me to pull a hamstring—it had been a while since I'd last moseyed, and I really should have stretched a little beforehand. The girl at the booth, wearing a smile the width of a draft horse's derriere, greeted us with a warm and friendly

"Howdy!" This threw me a little. I hadn't seen the "Howdy!" coming and was totally unprepared for it. As a result—and I'm embarrassed to confess this—I totally messed up my first "Howdy" of the Stampede.

You see, I had already begun to say "Hello," but midway into my "Hello," upon hearing her "Howdy!" I attempted to veer off into a "Howdy" myself, causing my face to contort into a painful, constipated expression, and the "Howdy" came out sounding like "Hell-o-o-o-dy-o-d-o-od-oudy." It sounded like something a coyote caught in a leghold trap might say, and the woman looked at me as though I was from Toronto. Sigh.

Moseying away as quickly as my pulled hamstring would allow, we headed to the premier event of the Stampede: pigeon racing. We arrived just as the pigeon master was telling the audience, and I quote, "These are the same pigeons used in both World War I and II!"

"Wow," I whispered to Two Nose, "they must be very old pigeons."

After a ten-minute later-than-expected arrival, some pigeons started to return to base. However, much to the crowd's amusement, rather than returning to the pigeon coop, they landed atop a beer truck.

"They must be Canadian," I whispered.

Next stop: the famous Clydesdale horses, where you could meet each one individually and learn their names. Most had tough-sounding names, the kind you would expect for a heavy draft horse, names like Thunder and Turbo. Then, suddenly, there was Steve. Obviously the nerd of the group, I explained to Two Nose.

We strolled into another agricultural building. Here you could guess the number of eggs in a box and win valuable prizes (read *eggs*), watch tiny piglets suckling their mom, meet a cow named Moaning Myrtle, and play a fun game called Find the Sick Animal. There was even a "pig poop cycle" display. (Thankfully), you don't see that every day.

Afterwards we watched a cow-milking demo, put on—I'm not making this up—by a fellow with the last name Pullman. Now, as a big fan of the old TV show *Green Acres*, I was hoping to watch Pullman yank on the cow's teats and get sprayed in the face, or perhaps have the cow knock over the metal bucket. Alas, in this high-tech age, he merely strapped onto

?

The amount of manure removed from the Agriculture Barn
would be about 15 kilometres long if piled 3 metres high by 2.5
metres wide. (Ever wonder who takes the time to figure out stuff
like this?)

the poor thing some very cold-looking tubes attached to a
machine you'd never want to encounter in your doctor's office.

Next we took part in the number one Stampede activity:
strolling aimlessly around the grounds, looking lost, hot, and
a little confused as to what to do next. We passed by a booth
doing a booming business selling Billy-Bob Teeth, and a llama
wearing a Tilley hat. We also spied a lot of small children teth-
ered to their parents on long bungee-cord-style leashes. This
seemed like an odd, yet I suppose effective, way of keeping
track of the wee ones.

We passed by the always popular bingo hall, which made
me ponder, "Does bingo cause smoking, or does smoking
cause you to play bingo?" Then we came to the carnival
games, where you can spend upwards of $300 trying to win
a $12.95 stuffed animal for your daughter. I tried my hand at
Whack-a-Mole, hoping to hold on to my world title, but fell
short in both qualifying heats. I blame it on the cowboy
boots.

My hamstring pull now fully recovered, we moseyed on over
to the rides, where roughly eight thousand people were lined
up to participate in assorted thirty-five-second-long rides.
When I was sixteen and much smarter than I am now, I would
spend eight hours straight riding on the same nauseating ride.
Now, a mere glance at half these rides is enough to send me
racing for the Pepto-Bismol.

Here are two fun activities to try if you don't like going on
the actual rides. First, you can steal the shoes of people enjoying the rides after they fall off and plummet to the earth.
(Allow me to clarify: I mean after the shoes fall off people's feet,
not after the *people* plummet to the earth.) Second, you can
play a little betting game I like to call Spot the Next Person

Who's Going to Barf. Ah, the Stampede fun never stops.

We strolled past the Carnival Diablo World of Wonder, housing, among other oddities, a mermaid, mummified prospector, and elephant man. The sign promised entrants "A hundred years of twisted humanity preserved for your own consumption." (Like I don't get enough of that at family reunions.)

Now, here's where I made the most serious error in judgment of the entire Stampede. Yes, even more serious than downing those seven corndogs. I suggested to my wife, no forced her, really—all in the name of fun, you understand—to participate in the old "guess your age or weight and win a prize" booth. Men, if you value your marriage in *any* way, please stay away from this booth. Enough said.

Two hours later, when old Two Nose began speaking to me again, we moseyed on over to a border collie demo and watched this frighteningly intelligent dog herd a family of ducks. I can't even get my own dog to fetch me the paper.

Approximately two and a half truckloads of horse manure are dropped along the Stampede Parade route.

Next, it was the mini-donkey races, where nicely dressed gentlemen, and a few ladies, sat atop mini-carts being pulled by mini-donkeys. They didn't go very fast, being, you know, mini and all, but it was cute, in a way that only a mini-donkey race could be.

Of course, no Stampede visit would be complete without seeing the Superdogs, where dogs of all shapes and sizes and breeds, along with their owners of all shapes and sizes and breeds, race against one another (the dogs, not the owners) through a maze of jumps and tunnels. It's the Olympics for dogs and, for a lot of folks, the highlight of the entire Stampede. People go nuts over the Superdogs. Why, I'm not sure. But I have this vision of people going back to their own lazy, overweight, untrained dogs and giving them a stern lecture about unfulfilled potential.

Cowboy poetry awaited us after the Superdogs extravaganza. Cowboy poetry is truly one of the great Albertan cultural treasures. There are cowboy poetry festivals all over the province. If you've never been to one, I urge you to saddle up and attend. The poems range from the touching to the dramatic to the sublime to the ridiculous. I, naturally, am most partial to the ridiculous, like the poems on this particular evening that touched on topics such as manure spreaders or cow flatulence.

Finally it was off to the rodeo, where real cowboys and cowgirls participate in activities that, for the most part, they never would have actually done in the old wild, wild west. I mean, really, weren't they a little too busy to suddenly stop working and say "Hey, Bob, why don't you all jump on that bull's back and see what happens?"

Watching the bull riding, one can't help but wonder about the mental condition of the very first person who thought it would be a good idea to jump aboard. Presumably, these are the same breed of folks who invent bungee jumping or stick metal objects into electrical outlets "just to see what happens."

One thing that struck me during the rodeo events was just how appropriate some competitors' names were. There was no Giddie Up 'der Pardner out there, I tell you. These were real cowboys, with real cowboy names, names that likely predetermined their future from birth, names like Spunk, Rowdy, Blue, and Cash.

After the rodeo, exhausted and corndogged out, we dragged our weary dogs back to the old ranch. As I rode my Honda off the back porch, as the sun set in the western sky, I could hear the sound of a timber wolf howling in the distance (okay, so it was someone's poodle barking—work with me here, folks) and somehow I just knew that the Greatest Outdoor Show on Earth would be around for a very long time. (Unless of course, someone decides it should all be moved indoors, which would really, really, as the cowboys say, "Suck eggs.")

Here's a Calgary insult to try on fellow Stampeders next year: You're all Stampede hat and no cattle.

things you really ought to know about alberta

On 9 December 2000, Northlands Spectrum in Edmonton created the world's largest Christmas cake log. It weighed 2,502 kilograms and was 21.95 metres long.

With 140 or so regularly scheduled bingo games a year, Wildwood, east of Edmonton, claims to be the "Bingo Capital of Canada."

The world's largest ice cream sundae was created by Palm Dairies Ltd. in Edmonton on 24 July 1988. It weighed 24.9 tonnes.

the magic spot

If only Alberta was that lucky . . .

I f you're going to call yourself a real Albertan, you best be running right now to take in the tour of the provincial legislature building in Edmonton. And if you've lived in Edmonton all your life but never bothered to take the tour, please, do so now. Tell them I sent you and you may even get in for free. (Okay, so it's free all the time—that's just one more reason to take in the tour.)

Now some of you, particularly from Calgary, might be whining, "Why does Edmonton get to have the legislature building and why does Edmonton get to call itself the City of

Champions, and why does Edmonton get to stay up so late?"

The answer to the first part of your whine is simple, really. Edmonton is home to the legislature building because Edmonton is the capital of the province. And, for whatever reason, it has been a long-standing Canadian tradition to place the government legislature building right in the capital. I know, I know, it seems silly, but there you have it.

Ah, but why *is* Edmonton the capital of Alberta? Good question.

Many communities lobbied long and hard for the honour, including not just the obvious Calgary, but other less likely contenders, including Banff, Cochrane, Lacombe, Medicine Hat, Blackfalds, Wetaskiwin, Red Deer, Athabasca Landing, and Vegreville.

With a population of only seventy-eight at the time, Vegreville based many of its arguments on its climate. It had more ozone, they argued. Moreover, because Vegreville was well beyond the reach of chinooks, horse-drawn sleighs wouldn't get bogged down in all the chinook-induced slushy slush. Banff argued it could best be fortified in a time of war, while Athabasca Landing used its proximity to the geographical centre of the province as its selling point. I'm not sure what Red Deer's arguments were—I suspect they had to do with the plentitude of good places to fuel up and grab some doughnuts for the road.

Of course, as the most populous city in the province, Calgary was a likely contender. It was not to be, as the decision was a political one. Calgary had sent Tories off to Ottawa at a time of a ruling Liberal prime minister. Edmonton, on the other hand, although only about half Calgary's size, supported the Liberals and thus was bestowed with West Edmonton Mall and capital status, although I'm not sure which came first. (See how much more progressive we are politically a century later? Can you imagine in this day and age a city or province being penalized for not supporting the federal Liberals?)

There's still hope for Calgary, though. Edmonton is only a *provisional* capital, which means it can be changed at any time with a major vote. If enough people get pissed at Edmonton, for example because it's really cold there one winter and no one wants to do business with the government in the capital city anymore because it's just too cold, the capital

?

Around 1895, Calgary's motto and rallying cry for why *it* should be considered the capital of Alberta was "Calgary, the Denver of Canada: its adaptability as a health resort and as a site for the Dominion sanatorium for the treatment of consumptives."

could be moved to Canmore—the sunny banana belt of the Rockies—where no one would ever complain about having to come and do business.

The other reason Calgarians can be slightly optimistic is that the building is partially supported by Calgary-area sandstone. And rumour has it the stone is beginning to erode. Ironic or what?

For now, Edmonton is the mother ship of the province, and rightfully so, because that's where the legislature building is located. Wouldn't it be a little strange to have the legislature building somewhere other than the capital? Of course, it also makes sense to have the seat of government as close as possible to the world's largest shopping mall, since governments do seem to enjoy their shopping.

So, as I said at the onset, it is imperative that a true Albertan visit the legislature at least once. After all, this is where your hard-earned tax dollars end up. What if there was nothing more than a giant arcade and waterslide inside the building? Wouldn't you want to reassure yourself, first-hand? And maybe go for a few slides?

The Alberta Legislature, I'm pleased to report back to you, does not house a waterslide, primarily because it was built between 1907 and 1912, prior to waterslide technology. It truly is, though, a magnificent building. Having been in most legislature buildings across Canada (I'm a bit of a groupie), I have to admit that this is perhaps the nicest one I've visited thus far, and likely a far cry from where the Alberta government originally met, namely the Thistle Ice and Roller Rink. (I'm not making this up. You can ask the nice tour guides they provide at no extra charge.)

Walking into the foyer, I was immediately impressed by the

expansive rotunda (no, I'm not talking about Ralph), which houses more than 2,000 tonnes of marble from Quebec. There are also statues of Princess Louise Caroline Alberta and Chief Crowfoot, as well as a stunningly beautiful fountain built in 1959 to honour the first visit of Queen Elizabeth II. It is all very elegant and dignified—in other words, not at all what you'd expect if you watch the sessions on a regular basis on television.

The Grand Staircase leads to the third floor (the rotunda being level two of the building) and to the main doors into the Legislative Assembly Chamber. Climbing the staircase, I couldn't help but wonder if some politicians slide down the banister when no one is looking. I asked the tour guide about this. As far as she knew, they were more inclined to go skinny dipping in the fountain.

The wooden doors leading into the assembly chamber are hand-carved out of red mahogany from Belize. Above the massive doors sits the Alberta Coat of Arms, also carved from mahogany. The Alberta Coat of Arms features a beaver to represent Canada, a lion to represent Britain, and a pronghorn to represent southern Alberta. To represent northern Alberta, there's, um, oh yeah—nothing. Sorry, folks. Maybe next time.

We strolled past the northeast wall along the third floor, which features portraits of past premiers. Ralph's portrait isn't there because he has yet to pass. But the others are all there, including our first premier . . . I'll give you a few minutes to think of his name . . . I know you know it . . . starts with "R" . . . rhymes with "mutherford" . . . yes, you've got it, Rutherford! Alexander Rutherford. Over there, there's our longest-serving premier, Ernest Manning, who held office from 1943 to 1968.

My wife and I noticed a few strange things about the portraits. First, they were all white males! What are the odds? We also noticed that the last two premiers (Getty and Lougheed) both played for the Edmonton Eskimos. (Incidentally, it's fun to tell Americans we've had two Eskimos for premiers.) Finally, my wife noticed how much many of them resembled old actors, such as David Niven and Christopher Plummer. (Unless my Alberta history is a little shaky, and David and Christopher actually were our premiers?)

After touring by the portraits of the Lieutenant Governors,

we stopped at the Mace display. At one time, the Mace was used to bonk MLAs on the head who just wouldn't shut up during sessions. Nowadays it plays more of a symbolic role, representing the ultimate symbol of authority wielded in the assembly.

They were in a bit of a time crunch when the first Mace was built, so Rufus E. Butterworth (isn't *that* a great name?), a CPR employee, became known as Alberta's first recycler by building the Mace in only a few weeks using nothing but recycled scrap materials. Plumbing pipe mounted on a toilet tank float functioned as the shaft, with old shaving mug handles serving as decorative bits around the orb. Parts of an old bedstead, scraps of wood, a piece of red velvet, and a coat of gold paint finished the job. Even though the "junkyard Mace" was meant to be temporary, it was used for fifty years.

The new Mace, built in 1955, is more elegant looking, but for me, somehow lacks the original model's folksy charm. The new Mace does have one unique feature: the names of the gems encircling the crown spell out Alberta:

Amethyst
Lapis lazuli
Beryl
Emerald
Ruby
Topaz
Aquamarine
Neat, eh?

The Mace display also featured the ceremonial sword used by the Sergeant-at-Arms until 1987, when a new sword was donated, and the Black Rod, which the Sergeant-at-Arms uses when escorting the Lieutenant Governor into the chamber. To prompt the opening of the chamber doors, the Black Rod is tapped gently three times on the doors at the start of each sitting of the legislature. After the three taps, the premier, from the other side of the doors, will say "Who's there?" in a voice eerily reminiscent of Ricky Ricardo, prompting a giggling fit from the entire gaggle of MLAs. Upon which time, the doors will be opened.

We strolled up to the fourth floor, walking past portraits of King George V and Queen Mary, the ruling monarchs when the legislature opened. After walking through the metal detector and forfeiting my slingshot to the kindly security guard, we entered the galleries overlooking the chamber. It was exciting to watch our government in action, to be a witness to lofty ideas being debated purely on their intellectual merits, and to see the collegial nature that existed among all government members, regardless of party affiliation. Here's a taste of the debate we sat through:

Tory MLA: "Make me."

Opposition MLA: "You make me, eggplant face."

Tory MLA: "I know you are, but what am I?"

Opposition MLA: "Make me."

Tory MLA: "No, you make *me*, poo-poo head."

Opposition MLA: "No, you're the poo-poo head."

And on and on it went. Those of us in the galley who were still awake were completely riveted.

Actually, I'm making that up. We'd missed the sitting, so the chamber was completely devoid of any constructive debate, as usual. (I came up with that realistic dialogue based on the many exchanges I've seen on television, in case you're wondering how I could have so accurately portrayed a session.)

The chamber includes a mind-boggling 620 light bulbs and offers seating for about 215 spectators, including special guests and members of the press. However, the press usually prefers to watch the festivities on television from the basement, where there are no windows or air, but where they do get thrown the odd scrap of bread.

The tour guide pointed out where special guests such as ambassadors sit, prompting my wife to say, "Did you say 'That's where the bastards sit?'" An uproarious giggling fit among the other tour participants ensued.

Looking into the Chamber, we could see how, owing to their massive majority, many of the sitting Tories had to bring in their own lawn chairs. We also learned that the distance between the opposition side and government side is exactly two arm lengths, plus two and a half sword lengths, to prevent any fights from breaking out. (Sadly, this distance does little to prevent spitball attacks from either side of the house.)

Next, it was time for the much-anticipated "magic spot," discovered accidentally by a maintenance worker, and now identified by a small gold circular plate in the hallway of the fourth level. Step onto the magic spot and suddenly, owing to a quirk of architecture and sound waves bouncing off the ceiling to this very spot, it sounds as though you've just stepped into the rotunda fountain. Step a few inches away from the magic spot, and the sound level drops off immediately and substantially. This alone was worth the price of admission, which, as I said, was free.

We signed the guest book before leaving, noticing the many signatures from around the world. There were pages upon pages of eloquent comments from visitors hailing from Japan, Italy, Australia, and Germany, plus one "Grooooooovy, baby!" from someone in Lethbridge. This proved yet again that people from Lethbridge should not be allowed near guest books or, for that matter, out of Lethbridge.

Having walked the hallowed halls of government, we left the building feeling a little more patriotic, a little more Albertan, and a lot more hungry—they don't even have an ice cream parlour or hot dog stand inside. If the capital ever does get moved from Edmonton to Canmore, I'm lobbying for at least a french fry stand.

And maybe, just maybe, a waterslide.

What do you call a Liberal in Alberta?
Lost.

What happens when two Liberals meet up in Calgary?
We don't know, it's never happened.

First man: "Two Liberals walk into a Calgary bar ... "
Second man: "What is this, a joke or something?"

What's the easiest way to get elected in Alberta if you're a Conservative?
Make sure your name appears on the ballot.

Why did the Albertan cross the road?
To get to the *right* side.

———————————

A guy strolls into a bar in Longview and shouts, "All Conservatives are a bunch of horses' asses!"

The bar patrons mob the poor fellow and beat him up.

After the man recovers, he goes back into the same bar, only this time he shouts, "All Liberals are a bunch of horses' asses!"

Again, the poor fellow is mobbed and beaten.

He goes back into the bar a third time, screams "All NDPers are a bunch of horses' asses!" and this time gets beaten to a pulp.

Later, while recovering at the hospital, the poor fellow asks the doctor, "I just don't get it, who *do* these people vote for?"

"You don't understand," the doctor replies. "This is *horse* country."

a humorist's guide to alberta politicians

S ince we've just visited our fair province's seat of power, it
seems fitting that we now have a quick offbeat review of
some Alberta politicians who have made a name for themselves in recent years.

For the non-Albertans who are *not* from Prince Edward
Island, let's start with a simple test:

Question 1: Name three politicians from PEI.

Question 2: Name three politicians from Alberta.

Chances are you named Anne of Green Gables for question
1, which is partially incorrect. For question 2, you likely earned
bonus points by rattling off at least five Alberta politicians.

You see, Alberta politicians may be known for a lot of different things, but at least they are known. Most of them, from a
humour perspective, have scored high marks over the years
for their innate ability to enrich Canada's comedic landscape.

Joe Clark

Joe who? Joe Clark. Joe who? Joe Clark, that's who. The former prime minister from High River, Alberta (the first true
Albertan prime minister), was known for his decency, lost lug-
gage, and inability to add up votes in the House of Commons
before voting on important things, like, oh say, the federal
budget. Joe was the antithesis of Brian Mulroney, at least
chin-wise.

During the 2000 federal election, Joe rode into the heart of
Reform/Alliance country in Calgary and won a seat as the
leader of the Progressive Conservative party. He did this with
the help of a catchy billboard campaign featuring a frighten-

ingly massive photo of his face and the slogan "More than just a pretty face." Joe's self-effacing humour scored a lot of points in Alberta, where we tend not to do self-effacing humour.

In his dying days of politics, Joe was branded a traitor for his quasi-support in the 2004 federal election of the Liberals over the Conservatives. All the self-effacing humour in the world wouldn't save him from that call in Alberta.

Stockwell Day

The former Alberta provincial finance minister karate-kicked his way into the leadership role of the Alliance after delegates decided that vision and policy ideas were vastly overrated. Stockwell jet-skied his way into the history books, arriving in a wetsuit at his first press conference on the shore of Okanagan Lake, BC. This precipitated chaos among the political satire community after it was overwhelmed with the generous gift presented to it.

Rick Mercer gave a further boost to Stockwell's comedy quotient by launching a recall vote on the Web, petitioning people to vote for Stockwell Day to change his name to Doris Day, as a way to highlight potential problems with the party's pro-referendum policy position.

Stockwell/Doris, in an effort to boost tourism to Alberta's dinosaur country, once claimed to believe that dinosaurs and people roamed Earth at the same time. After working for the government, and being a keen observer of Canadian politics, I have to say that I now agree with Doris 100 percent.

Deborah Grey

Ms. Grey entered federal politics as the first Reform Member of Parliament. Voted Most Likely to Be Someone's Aunt, Deborah's fondness for motorcycles and leather made her a memorable addition to the House. She'll be missed from question period primarily because of her frequent use of the word "pot-licker." (I'm not making this up—it really was her favourite heckle.)

Stephen Harper

Stephen Harper is, at the time of writing, the Federal Leader of Her Majesty's Official Opposition and the leader of the Conservative Party of Canada. Harper was once part of a small

177

posse of Albertans calling for Alberta to build a firewall around the province, which I think was intended to help maintain Alberta's rat-free status.

Stephen's most frightening comedic moment was when he planted a rather firm lip-lock on ace reporter Marg Delahunty (Mary Walsh of _This Hour Has 22 Minutes_), surfacing for air with lipstick smeared all over his face. He has also demonstrated some ability to laugh at himself by joking that he became an economist because he didn't have the charisma to be an accountant. Word has it he's also known to do a mean impersonation of both Jean Chrétien and Brian Mulroney.

After moving into Stornoway—the Official Opposition residence in Ottawa—his wife Laureen joked that they should build a fire pit in the backyard so they can sit around the fire and drink beer, the way folks do in Alberta. I truly wished they'd followed through with this idea—I've been complaining for years that what Ottawa really needs is a good weenie roast.

In 2003, Stephen Harper united the political right in a lovely wedding featuring Peter Mackay as the nervous bride and David Orchard as the jilted lover.

Preston Manning

Son of former Alberta premier Ernest Manning, Preston picked up his papa's political reins and founded the Refoooooooooorm Party, largely out of frustration with Jean Chrétien's, Brian Mulroney's, Pierre Trudeau's, and John A. Macdonald's federal policies. Preston almost single-handedly mobilized conservative forces in the west. Most impressive of all, he once received an image makeover from those _Queer Eye for the Straight Guy_ guys (or maybe the makeover was on _Oprah_, I can't remember now).

Not to be outdone in the self-effacing humour category, Preston tried his hand (and did very well, I might add) as a stand-up comic on an _Open Mike with Mike Bullard_ show and made appearances on the _Royal Canadian Air Farce_, poking fun at himself. "Can you say Refoooooooooooooooooorm?"

Myron Thompson

Perhaps the quintessential Alberta politician. Myron is often the only Canadian MP regularly photographed wearing a large white cowboy hat and bolo tie, looking decidedly like he just rolled out of the old bunkhouse. Myron would have made a wonderful sheriff for any Alberta town about 120 years ago.

Myron has represented Wild Rose riding as a federal MP four terms, first with the Reform Party, then the Alliance, and now the Conservatives. A true "cowboy of the people," Myron has consistently managed to rack up more votes each election than almost any other elected official in Canada. During another landslide victory in 2004, news anchor Lloyd Robertson described Myron as, and I quote, "That guy with the big white cowboy hat." Yup. That's our Myron.

Ralph

Ralph Klein is the longest-serving premier in Canada. And, like Madonna, Cher, or Fabio, he's the only Canadian politician who routinely goes by his first name only.

Owing to his shyness in front of the cameras, many eastern Canadians may not have a true appreciation of King Ralph, so here are several things out-of-province folks ought to know about our ruling monarch. In fact, I'm going to make a little more room here for Ralph, since King Ralph has definitely earned his political humour stripes.

Fun Facts About Ralph

- As a child Ralph would sneak into the drive-in theatre with his buddies and eat mustard and ketchup packets as snacks. (This explains a lot, although what exactly, I'm not sure.)

- Ralph was a weatherman for a short while, a career that helped mould his sense of fashion.

- Ralph began his career as a journalist, the perfect starter career for a politician, providing him with all the training he needs to answer questions without actually answering questions.

- When he was mayor of Calgary, he once made a vague comment about "bums and creeps" coming from out east and filling up Calgary jails, but he meant it in a nice way, even travelling out east to tell them to their faces, which earned Mayor Ralph huge bonus points back in Cowtown.

- He once advocated the use of "cowboy techniques" to control undesirables, thus cementing his reputation as a true-blue Albertan.

- His third run at mayordom, in 1986, saw Ralph win 93 percent of the votes, numbers that even North Korea would have a hard time running up.

- He was once quoted as saying "You sort of think that when Louis Riel was fighting for his territory, he didn't have Edmonton in mind." Approval ratings in Calgary skyrocketed.

- Ralph caused three car accidents on icy Calgary streets while waving at passing motorists during his first campaign for provincial MLA.

- He only got a C on a paper he wrote while taking a Mount Royal College communications program. Ironically, the paper's title was "How to Win an Election."

- His presence in politics spawned the creation of several new words, including Ralphenomenon, Ralpherendum, Ralphonomics, and the Ralphinator.

- During a provincial election campaign, Ralph poked fun at Laurence Decore's statement about harnessing energy from cow flatulence by publicly asking how the Liberals planned to get all the cows to fart at the same time.

- To this day (this day currently being a Tuesday), he reportedly signs all official government documents simply "Premier Ralph."

So there you have it. Your complete guide to all things Ralph, and your incomplete guide to Alberta's politicians. I'd now love to get into a satirical political discourse on the ins and outs of Alberta politics in general, particularly on Alberta's role in confederation and tenuous relationship with Ottawa, but I'd like to keep this puppy to under ten thousand pages and spare a couple of rainforests.

Why doesn't Red Deer have a professional hockey team?
Response if you're an Edmontonian: Because then Calgary would want one too.
Response if you're a Calgarian: Because then Edmonton would want one too.

―――――――――――――

What's the best thing to come out of Edmonton?
Response if you're a Calgarian: Highway 2 south to Calgary.

―――――――――――――

What's the best thing to come out of Calgary?
Response if you're an Edmontonian: Highway 2 north to Edmonton.

―――――――――――――

What's the best way to really enjoy Edmonton?
Response if you're a Calgarian: Stop your trip at Sylvan Lake.

―――――――――――――

What's the best way to really enjoy Calgary?
Response if you're an Edmontonian: Stop your trip at Sylvan Lake.

―――――――――――――

A Calgary-based company was giving out prizes to Calgarians: free roundtrip airline tickets and accommodation in Edmonton. First prize was one week, second prize two weeks, third prize an entire month.

the battle of alberta

"It is imperative to praise Edmonton in Edmonton, but it is sudden death to praise it in Calgary."
—Poet Rupert Brooke

E dmonton. Calgary. (Sorry, I've just offended the Calgarians. Let me start over.)

Calgary. Edmonton. (Now I've pissed off the Edmontonians. You see, you just can't win in Alberta.)

The Edmonton–Calgary rivalry, or, as some call it, the Calgary–Edmonton rivalry, has been a part of the fabric of Alberta since this great province was first stitched together. It all goes back to when an early pioneer named Gus Holbrook from Calgary borrowed fifty dollars from an Edmonchuck settler named Hugh Munger, and then Hugh's younger sister ran off with a Calgarian named Bill Buck, who had been married to an Edmontonian named Cecile Langois, who was cousin to one Russ Porter, who had that very day stolen a mare from Gus Holbrook, whose father, coincidentally, had just been kicked in the head by a cow that hailed from Calgary.

Anyway, that's the rumour. Since that time, the two cities have fought like cats and dogs, trading barbs back and forth with the vicious ferociousness of a Jerry Springer show. They've ignored each other, laughed at each other's misfortunes, even gone to war. Well, not so much war as played hockey. Which, in Canada, is almost the same thing.

Just one example of how crazy the rivalry has been: in 1913, when the competition between the Calgary Tigers and

Edmonton Eskimos was so intense, they had to hold their games in neutral Red Deer.

Battle of the Slogans

Edmonton slogans: "City of Champions," "We're Still the City of Champions!", 'Really, We're Still the City of Champions!', "Have You Been to Our Mall Yet?" and "Hey—At Least We're Not Calgary!"

vs.

Calgary slogans: "Calgary—It'll be a Great City When It's Finished!", "Calgary—The Friendly Neighbour By-Law Capital of Canada!", Calgary—Gateway to Canmore" and "Hey—At Least We're Not Edmonton!"

It's easy to see why the rivalry persists so fervently. Like siblings in a volatile, emotional family, ignored by parents who spent all their time coddling the kids back east, these kids grew up in the same household, maturing into roughly the same-sized, evenly matched adult urban centres of Alberta they are today.

Here's a small sample of the scorecard often used to compare the two cities:

Edmonton	**Calgary**
Capital of Alberta	Presumed capital of southern Alberta if southern Alberta ever separates
West Edmonton Mall: The Greatest Indoor Show in Earth	Calgary Stampede: The Greatest Outdoor Show on Earth
Fringe Festival, with bizarre performance artists and plenty of laughs	Town council meetings, with bizarre performance artists and plenty of laughs

what's so <u>funny</u> about alberta?

Edmonton	Calgary
Receives plenty of hot air from politicians at legislature	Receives plenty of hot air from chinooks
Known for the arts	Known for business (which makes the money to pay for all the arts)
Home to the Fantasyland Hotel	Nice Motel Six near the airport
Home of the largest western boot in Canada	Home of the Calgary Tower
Nice view of the far north	Nice view of the mountains
Lots of government workers	Lots of cowboys
13.8 percent rate of obesity	14.5 percent rate of obesity
Hosted the 1978 Commonwealth Games	Hosted the 1988 Winter Olympics
Created the world's largest Yule cake	Second-biggest consumers of Slurpees in the world
Top city for horse-race betting in the world	Top city for fake horse-race betting (courtesy the St. Louis Hotel)
Had Wayne Gretzky	Didn't have Wayne Gretzky

And on and on the list could go, with endless and meaningless comparisons being tossed back and forth until someone finally says, "I've had it. I'm moving to Red Deer." (This is in fact why so many people live in Red Deer.)

The important things to know for the new Albertan who has just arrived in the hopes of weaseling their way into our hard-earned surplus dividend money is this:

1. Never say anything nice about Calgary while visiting Edmonton.
2. Never say anything nice about Edmonton while visiting Calgary.
3. Never say anything about anything while visiting Red Deer.

If you follow these three simple rules, you should live a long and healthy Albertan life. Even if you are from Saskatchewan (which is a whole other rivalry that I don't have time to get into).

And for everyone out there, Albertan and non-Albertan, Edmontonian and Calgarian alike, remember this: like two mature siblings who have grown up alongside each other through thick and thin, through hailstorms and tornadoes, through Stanley Cups and Grey Cups, through the National Energy Program and the mad cow crisis, deep down inside, though it's hard to see it sometimes, Calgary and Edmonton really do love each other. If they could just take that love and work together, just imagine . . . ah, hell, who am I kidding? Anyone up for a road trip to Red Deer?

During the 2004 Flames playoff hockey run, many Edmontonians still clung to the old "anyone but Calgary" mentality. But one Edmontonian, Reverend Neil Gordon of the St. Matthias Church, made news after placing a sign outside his church that read:

JESUS SAID WE SHOULD PRAY FOR OUR ENEMIES
GO FLAMES GO

an alberta shopping list

A lberta is now officially debt-free. So now it's rat-free, PST-free, *and* debt-free. What's not to love about Alberta?

Of course, now the government has a huge dilemma, namely, how to spend all that glorious money, Does it put the money aside in a rainy day fund like Norway or Alaska has done with their surpluses (practical, but boring)? Do they reduce taxes even further to attract business to Alberta (practical, yet somehow, hmmm, boring)? Or do they spend like a bunch of drunken Liberals suffering from a 70s flashback?

My vote: Spend! Spend like there's no tomorrow. Spend like you're Elton John inside the world's largest shoe store with a blank cheque in your hand. Spend before the Feds come for our money. Spend before the other provinces start lining up to our hefty teats. Forget this ridiculous notion about saving for future generations. After all, how do we know there will even *be* future generations? And how do we know they will be fiscally responsible? Better to spend it now, I say, than let some nebulous future generation blow it all on booze and hookers.

Ah, but *how* to spend? Much debate will ensue about what our priorities for investment ought to be. Sure, we could invest it in wise things that look toward the future, like wind power or education, or we could reduce waiting times for hip replacement surgery by four years, but why would any reasonable government all of a sudden, completely out of the blue, begin spending our money wisely?

So, here then, is my personal Alberta Advantage shopping list of the top ten ways I'll be urging our government to spend the surpluses:

Top Ten Ways Alberta Should Blow Its Wad

10. Buy every Albertan a hat, but not just *any* hat—a really, really *cool* hat.

9. Purchase Saskatchewan once and for all and be done with it. (I mean, how much could it cost, really? You know they're just waiting for it.)

8. Invest in more gigantic roadside attractions so that we ensure no Alberta community is left behind.

7. Please, for the love of God, fix the pothole on the corner of my street.

6. Buy every Albertan their very own cow to help support the beef industry.

5. Free lifetime passes to everyone for the submarine rides at West Edmonton Mall.

4. Buy a couple of Senate seats. (Let's face it, the only way Alberta is going to fulfill its dream of getting a few elected Albertan senators in the Senate is by greasing a few palms.)

3. Build a state-of-the-art research facility dedicated to studying the brainwaves of people who eat spray-on cheese.

2. Expand Calgary's Plus 15 sidewalk system all the way to Edmonton.

1. Purchase a small state of our choice and turn it into a theme park. Just because we could, if we wanted to.

the trip north

"Have you heard the weather forecast for Grande Prairie?" asked the man seated next to me, a trace of concern in his voice.

"No, why?" I asked, momentarily forgetting my rule about never asking people why.

"Because I heard there's a huge system sitting right on top of Grande Prairie. I'm surprised we're even taking off."

Those are the words you want to hear as your plane taxis down the runway—*I'm surprised we're even taking off.*

But take off we did. Unfortunately. Unfortunate because, for the flight's duration, our plane was at the mercy of 200-kilometre-per-hour chinook crosswinds blasting us from atop the Rockies. And since our flight path from Calgary to Grande Prairie took us directly along the mountain front, we would all enjoy the thrill of being tossed about like a fresh salad in the hands of a manic chimpanzee for the entire flight.

It truly was a roller-coaster ride from start to finish. In fact, the turbulence was so bad I spent most of the flight on the lap of the gentleman seated next to me. (Not because of the turbulence, but because I was scared out of my boxers and he seemed like a rather comforting sort of fellow.) At one point, we dipped so violently that a woman screamed like a hyena on uppers, adding to the festive, amusement park–like atmosphere.

"This is fun!" I said to my seatmate.

"You have a sick and disturbing idea of fun," he replied tersely.

"How did you know?" I replied.

Then things really went downhill. A child, not much older than six or seven, seated kitty corner from us, vomited. When I say "vomited," I mean it the same way a volcanologist might casually comment, "Krakatoa just blew." Since the air flow in the aircraft's "economy" section wasn't working properly, and the temperature was stifling hot, the vomit added a new, exciting element to the flight. The excitement escalated when the woman in front of me decided to join in with her own unique contribution.

"Looks like we're flying Air Barf," I said to the fellow next to me, who had now turned several shades of green, none of them very becoming.

With a look of steely determination in her eye and a wet cloth in her hand, the flight attendant strolled back to the plane's midsection, now affectionately dubbed the "barf class." This poor woman then squatted in the midst of the worst of the turbulence and began to sponge up the mess.

Cleaning up vomit isn't high on my list of fun things to do. Cleaning up vomit while being tossed like a sock in a dryer at 32,000 feet, for me, falls somewhere on the old fun scale between preparing my taxes and performing my own root canal.

Yet this flight attendant, in the middle of all this in-flight tension, suddenly leapt to her feet in a spontaneous Julie Andrews moment and with a huge smile on her face shouted out, "I love my job!" The plane erupted with laughter.

Despite the fact that the turbulence persisted, that we had to circle over Grande Prairie's airport for an additional thirty-five minutes, that we had several aborted landings, and that we eventually landed in fog so dense that even my taxi driver got lost going to my hotel, it is that moment of spontaneous humour and energy I will always remember (especially since I'd rather forget the rest of the experience). I don't know who the flight attendant was, but I'm guessing she was an Albertan. Because that's just the kind of people we are. People who, even when mopping up barf, still manage to have a good time.

A lot of Albertans, I've come to realize, believe that Edmonton is located in the far north. Especially southern Albertans.

Southern Canadians in general, who like to huddle close to the American border in the hopes of benefiting from the occasional Floridian breeze, have a difficult time grasping the concept of "the north." To them, places such as Thunder Bay, Prince George, and Edmonton represent the far north—rural hick towns where winter lasts three seasons and only the heartiest of explorers (or in Edmonton's case, shoppers) dare tread.

Of course, to the folks who live in the real far north and who know more polar bears than people, this southern bias is tremendously amusing. Like the company I once did a training workshop for in Edmonton. Based in Nunavut, this organization had chosen Edmonton as its *southern* escape destination for the winter. Now *those* people are northerners.

As my journey to the centre of Alberta reminded me, Edmonton isn't even halfway up the province. The *real* northern Albertans hang out in Fort Chipewyan (the oldest settlement in Alberta), on the edge of Wood Buffalo National Park, or in booming Fort McMurray ("Newfoundland's second largest city"), a city in a perpetual state of boom, a place I regrettably would not get a chance to visit on this trip.

Real northern Albertans also hang their hats in towns such as Rainbow Lake, High Level, or Indian Cabins, just shy of the Northwest Territories border. Again, regrettably, I couldn't make it quite that far north this time around. (If only my publisher had come through with that extra ten-thousand-dollar travel budget, sigh.)

But I did make it (barely it would seem, given the flight), to Peace River Country, which definitely qualifies as northern Alberta. (Sure, there aren't polar bears in Peace River Country, but hey, in fairness to me, this is Alberta and we don't have any polar bears, okay?)

I named my circle tour of Peace Country the Peace and Love Tour, and although I briefly considered putting flowers in my hair, I chose instead to just wave the peace sign a lot and look as cool and laid back as I possibly could. This was going to be rather difficult as the rental company had run out of vehicles, leaving me with a honking huge, very uncool van the size of a school bus and the colour of a 1970s rumpus room couch.

I began my tour of the Peace in Grande Prairie, as soon as my stomach had landed from the flight from hell. As I motored along Highway 43 west of Grande Prairie, waving the peace sign to my fellow travellers, I couldn't help but wonder how many folks learn the functions of all the different buttons on their rental vehicles while cruising along a busy highway at 150 kilometres per hour. Maybe it's just me. Let's hope so.

There were no speed limit signs along the divided highway, so it began to feel like Germany's autobahn, only with lots of pickup trucks. The countryside was a mosaic of farmlands and parkland; herds of bison were plentiful on either side of the highway. The northern prairie of the Peace represents the northernmost extension of the central plains of North America and contains the largest area of open parkland between central Alberta and the Arctic Ocean, so I'd anticipated a lot of this scenery. (I like to anticipate my scenery well in advance.) The sky seemed bigger up north, even bigger than in the south, which somehow helped me feel like I really was on a Peace and Love journey. Groovy, baby, groovy.

I tuned into Peace Country Country, 890 on the AM dial, and listened to a country singer pine for his love, who had legs the size of a giraffe. A sudden rainstorm, however, brought an end to the music—I have this rule that you should never listen to country music in the rain or you're liable to kill yourself.

A motorhome towing a gigantic trailer slowed everyone down to the point where it felt more like Alberta and less like the autobahn. Motorhome drivers are, in my estimation, frustrated sailors, who, especially in landlocked Alberta, purchase a motorhome as the next best thing to commanding their own vessel. And have you noticed that motorhome drivers tend to be older? It's as though we reach a certain point in our lives where we feel we should be able to drive something that's as many feet long as we are years old.

The storm thankfully had passed, and the sky was a brilliant blue. The radio back on, tuned now to the CBC, where I learned that 17.7 percent of Peace Country residents are overweight, which actually seemed quite low to me, especially since I'd just returned from a trip to Florida.

My first stop was in Beaverlodge, where, rumour had it, they were planning to erect the world's largest beaver as a roadside monument that would do justice to the town's name.

This, I knew, could lead to civil war in Alberta—Castor, in southern Alberta, *also* lays claim to a roadside beaver statue. It is my hope, however, that cooler heads will prevail and Castor will decide to spend its money not on weapons, but on the creation of an even larger beaver, thus setting off a sort of beaver arms race between Castor and Beaverlodge as they attempt to out-beaver each other.

Alas, the beaver was not yet erect. (It may just be me, but does that sentence read right?)

I popped into the town office to get the skinny on the beaver and discovered I was only a few days shy of the beaver's erection. The statue, featuring a beaver straddling a log, was to be placed along the highway bisecting Beaverlodge, with a ceremony befitting the erection of a large beaver.

I mentioned the possible rivalry with Castor to the woman behind the counter. With an evil glint in her eyes, she confided to me, in a rather conspiratorial tone, "I am very, very pleased that Beaverlodge's beaver is going to be substantially larger than Castor's beaver."

"How much larger?"

"Our beaver will be fifteen feet high," she proudly informed me, "whereas Castor's beaver is only five feet high."

She handed me an information sheet regarding the "Beaver Project," as it had been dubbed. The project's total cost from inception to mounting—around $40,000—was paid entirely from local donations. A smaller-scale model had been built as a sort of prototype, because, to quote the infor-mation sheet, "We want the beaver to look like a beaver." (This seemed like the kind of common-sense approach one would find commonplace throughout the north. After all, there is no sense having your beaver look like a hippo or a duck.) The information sheet also touted the success of Glendon's giant pyrogy, noting that "their pyrogy has been worth its weight in gold." Amen to that.

I interviewed a local resident who confided to me that although most folks were solidly behind the beaver, a few were worried that having the world's largest beaver was perhaps not the most appropriate claim to fame for a community. Then, after a brief bout of giggling, she leaned in to me and whis-pered another startling admission: "From the conceptual drawings I've seen, I'm a little concerned that it looks like the beaver is humping the log."

I told her not to worry, that either way it was a win for the town, and I was certain thousands of patriotic Albertans would enjoy the sight of our national animal so proudly displayed in all its glory, no matter what it was doing.

After all, as the beaver project information sheet said, if it worked with a pyrogy . . .

Now, before I leave my insightful analytical discussion of Beaverlodge, Alberta, I'd like to take this time to recognize it for its entrance sign, which proudly displays the basic facts that any travelling male over forty wants to know: "Population 2100, Elevation 2400." If I were premier of Alberta, I would enact a law requiring every community to post a sign declaring its vital statistics like this. Size and elevation, after all, are two burning things every male (it's genetically programmed) wants to know about every town he enters. Trust me on this one. It's more important to our sanity than you could ever imagine.

Beyond Beaverlodge, I encountered more bison, more elk farms, a few healthy-looking hogs, and a growing number of aspen trees. I also noticed a sign advertising an electric fence demonstration and wondered about the fun possibilities involved in such a demo: "Hey, Alvin, come here for a minute, I've got something neat to show you!"

I passed through Hythe, the "Town of Flowing Wells," which also doubles as the "Volunteer Capital of Canada." After turning off the highway, I puttered along the main drag of Hythe, past the Curl Up and Dye hair salon, and noticed that some roads in the village were not yet paved. I stopped in at the small tourist centre to ask how it was that the volunteer capital of Canada could still have unpaved roads, but it was closed. Where were all these volunteers when you needed them?

Back on the highway, and another storm rolled overhead. It had taken me only an hour or so to figure out how to use the rental van wipers, so I felt a bit more relaxed as I cruised past directional signs pointing to exotic-sounding places such as

Sexsmith and Gundy. One sign asked travellers to report all dinosaur sightings from Tumbler Ridge, BC, which made Tumbler Ridge sound very exciting. And either I wasn't paying attention (plausible), or there still was not a single speed limit sign to be seen along the highway. Peace Country was proving to be more wild and wooly than I'd expected. Groovy, baby.

At the town of Demmitt, someone had, rather predictably, crossed out "Demmitt" on the welcome sign and marked "DAMMIT" over top in bold, black letters. There wasn't much to see in Demmitt, damn it. It was sort of a one-horse town minus the one horse, so I headed on to beautiful British Columbia.

I know, I know, you're probably thinking, "What, is he nuts? Why would he leave Alberta?" I knew it was dangerous to cross the border, but I wanted to at least get a taste of BC for comparative reasons, so I could understand why it was that millions of British Columbians flee their homeland every year for our little piece of heaven. Besides, the only way to make the Peace and Love circle tour work was by zipping across the border and crossing back through Dawson Creek.

A huge black wall of foreboding clouds hung in the west-ward sky, lending a rather ominous feel to my imminent arrival in BC. The landscape was subtly changing, too—aspens giving way to ponds and stunted black spruce. Prime moose country. Groovy.

A sign announcing "Last Cheap Gas!" let me know I would soon be leaving the land of plenty. Then two things happened the exact moment I crossed into British Columbia, which is the way I always thought it should be when you cross a bor-der. Things should happen. Something, *anything*, should be different. There is nothing, after all, more anticlimactic than crossing a border and having everything look, feel, and smell the same as before. So I was glad two things clearly marked the occasion of my departure from Alberta.

The first was this: the highway improved considerably. I left behind rather rough, weathered pavement to find myself abruptly cruising silently along a swath of freshly laid highway pavement. This struck me as odd. Here I was leaving Canada's wealthiest province and entering a province that had recently been downgraded to "have-not" poorer cousin status. Perhaps BC blew its money on roads?

The second occurrence: the moment, and I do mean the moment, I crossed the boundary line, CBC Radio disappeared from the airwaves. It didn't just gradually fade away or die a slow mournful death within a few minutes of crossing the border. No, it died the nanosecond I crossed the provincial line, which at least added to the feeling that I had passed into a different world.

Then two more things of note, so really *four* things happened upon my border crossing. Groovy. There was a notice of a time change, which doesn't happen when you cross into BC in the southern half of the province. I must say I thoroughly enjoy passing through time zones because I figure it's the closest we'll ever get to actual time travel. And the fourth event: there were suddenly, finally, speed limit signs. (Man, are they draconian in BC or what?)

Driving toward Dawson Creek, I fumbled with the radio dial until I reconnected with the CBC, finding it hidden away farther down the dial. Only it was an hour earlier, prompting a massive case of déjà vu as I listened to the same stories and interviews I'd just heard, only I knew exactly how they would all end. Better yet, there was a phone-in contest, and I knew the answer to the question even before the announcers! I tried to figure out if I could phone in and win the prize, but my brain got sucked into a space-time continuum conundrum, which I found far too intellectually taxing, so I gave up on the whole idea.

Pulling into Dawson Creek, "Mile zero on the Alaska Highway," I noticed that gas was going for ten cents more per litre than in Alberta. I wasn't in Kansas anymore, Toto. The higher prices also reminded me of a news story from a few years back, when folks in this corner of BC were particularly pissed at one of their revolving door governments (I'm not sure which one it was—it's just too hard to keep track of all their premiers), and some people publicly mused about separating from BC and joining Alberta, whom they felt a stronger affinity with. This at a time when thousands of Saskatchewanians continued to flock into Alberta. Sigh. It's not easy being so popular and so beloved, but it is a cross we must bear in Alberta.

I could see why they wanted to join us. Sure, they had nice pavement and speed limit signs, but where was the cheap gas? Why did I have to pay a provincial sales tax on my Coffee Crisp? And where, pray tell, were the giant pyrogies and log-humping beavers? Where were the enormous Easter eggs and towering sausages? It was time to return to Alberta.

Circling back eastwards along Highway 49, I reentered Alberta some sixty minutes after I had left her, losing my gained hour in the process and once again returning immediately to less-than-stellar asphalt.

I must confess that after crossing the provincial boundary, it somehow just felt like Alberta again. Why, I have no idea. It just felt like home. *My god, am I becoming an Albertan?*

?

I passed the one-street town of Bay Tree and was relieved to see lower gas prices being advertised. Oh sure, higher gas prices might force us all to be more environmentally friendly and to stop driving those ridiculous Hummers and belching SUVs, but I was on a road trip, so, please, leave me alone.

There were speed limit signs along this stretch of the highway, and I noticed that the limit was now 100 kilometres per hour vs. only 90 kilometres per hour in BC. No wonder the poor bastards wanted to join us.

I drove by a moose and calf, several herds of bison, more elk farms, and a dog that I'm almost certain was the Littlest Hobo or, at the very least, Son of the Littlest Hobo.

A sign indicating 8 kilometres north to the town of Bonanza was all it took to plant the TV theme tune from *Bonanza* into my brain for at least the next hour. Of course, one can't help but hum the theme music from *Bonanza* without pretending to ride a horse, so it wasn't too long before I began to feel a little motion sick, bopping up and down on my seat in time to the music.

On through Spirit River, then Rycroft, then north onto Highway 2. Just past Rycroft I watched two cows—and I'm not making this up—wrestling with each other. The one cow seemed to have the other cow in a sort of bovine headlock. Things were getting strange up north. Groovy, baby. Peace and love.

A story on the radio about self-cleaning clothes dislodged the *Bonanza* theme song from my head, long enough for me to ponder if there would someday be self-cleaning diapers. Wouldn't *that* revolutionize the world? Of course, we'd all be in diapers until we were twelve, but still, it seemed like an idea of considerable merit.

A thunderstorm warning was in effect; lightning was putting on a dazzling show to the west. Alberta had had an unusual number of violent storms, hailstorms, and tornado warnings in 2004, prompting me to try to remember what it is a person should do in a severe lightning storm or tornado situation. Play dead? Or is that only with grizzlies? I should probably find out if I'm going to stay in Alberta.

The storm never materialized, and for the third time that day, the blue sky opened up in front of me, just as the road dramatically dipped down into the Peace River valley, which seemed to materialize out of nowhere. It was like the Grand Canyon of northern Alberta, a dramatic river gorge with the mighty and historic Peace River meandering lazily on by and a beautiful old blue highway bridge offering safe passage across.

It was peaceful up here in the Peace on my Peace and Love Tour, especially since I had the highway very much to myself, save for the odd trucker, farmer, or occasional RVer. Yes, Peace River Country definitely seemed to be a yuppie-free zone, with nary a minivan or SUV in sight.

But there were cows. Shortly after climbing out of the river valley, I spotted two cows trying to break into someone's cabin. (Again, let me stress, I'm not making this up.) The cows were on the porch, one of them ramming its head against the front door in a desperate attempt to gain entrance inside. The other, I suppose, was playing sentry by keeping a watchful eye out for anyone who might catch the would-be burglars in the act.

I tell you—the cows are strange up north. Very strange.

The Fairview Ski Hill was 6 kilometres to the west, or so the sign said. These Alberta prairie ski hills—and I've come across several of them in my travels—befuddle a mountain boy like me, mostly because the prairie landscape seems so utterly and completely devoid of mountains. Or even sometimes hills. Or for that matter bumps.

Turning off Highway 2 onto Highway 64 to Hines Creek,

there were about seventy-four advertising signs on posts plastering the corner at the junction. If a motorist stopped, pulled over, walked right up to the mass of signs, plunked his butt down into a lawn chair, and read them slowly, he might, with some patience, be able to read a few of the signs. Passing by at highway speed, all I was able to deduce was that there were things and stores and services and stuff—lots of stuff—in the general area, in case I should need any of those things, especially stuff. But my side trip to the village of Hines Creek was for one purpose and one purpose only—to have a gander at "The World's Largest Railway Spike."

Just before turning into Hines Creek, I spied a coyote with something large, and presumably dead, draped in its mouth. I was happy to see this—I've always had this theory that if the animals are eating well, it's probably good eatin' for humans too, and I was getting hungry.

A sign welcomed me to "The End of Steel" at Hines Creek, a reference to the fact that this is the end of the line for the Canadian National Railway in this neck of the woods. The End of Steel Museum had closed up shop for the day, leaving me with just the spike as my primary source of amusement.

The world's largest railway spike was easily found along the main street of Hines Creek. It sat on a small section of railway track in the centre of a small plot of grass. It was large, but not massive in a King Kong sort of way, more like just a very, very big spike, maybe 5 metres long, perhaps a little longer. So if you want to see a very, very big railway spike, go to Hines Creek. It could probably double for a very big nail, if that's more to your taste.

A whirlwind tour of Hines Creek revealed a fantastically western-looking saloon, the End of Steel Tavern, and two hair salons. For such a tiny place, this seemed excessive by about two. I popped into a local restaurant for a quick visit and suddenly felt like Michael Moore at a Bush family picnic. So although the coyote had turned my thoughts to food, I decided to press on.

Back onto my circle tour along Highway 2, as day one on my Peace and Love tour wound down, I tried to etch into my mind permanent memories of the towns and villages I was passing through. The dots on the map were quickly becoming real places:

First, the town of Fairview—"The Heart of the Peace"—where a young kid played with a yo-yo on the side of the highway.

Then Blue Sky. Clouds had rolled in again, but a small patch of blue sky opened up right above the town of Blue Sky, which freaked me out a little. Was it a setup? How could this be?

And at the village of Irwin (population 606), I found a small sandwich board sign in the middle of the main street, confirming its small-town status. (You see, I have this theory that for a town to qualify as being small, it must have at least one sandwich board sign right in the middle of its main street.)

Although it was getting late, I bypassed the direct route to Peace River, where I planned to spend the night, and opted for what I hoped was a more scenic route via the Peace River valley. Taking the secondary route of Highway 684, it quickly became apparent I'd made the right decision.

The road dropped steeply to the wide and very green banks of the Peace River. Farmhouses dotted the pastoral landscape. The Peace River runs over 1,500 kilometres from its headwaters in northeastern BC, cutting a swath across northern Alberta to Lake Athabasca. Yet it was hard to imagine that there was any other stretch of the river as beautiful as the one before me.

This was what I had anticipated from the Peace—the Eden-like countryside just oozed with a sense of abundance and fertility. It struck me as the kind of place where even a hopeless clod like me could learn to farm, a place where you could grow bananas or mangoes or any damn thing you pleased, and where babies arrived in bundles of three or four at a time—it was just that fertile looking.

Before heading north to Peace River, I dropped southward to the end of Highway 684, where the Shaftesbury ferry provided passage across the valley to the south side of the Peace River, linking up with another secondary highway in the middle of nowhere. I have always loved sailing, so I thought I'd take advantage of this rare Albertan opportunity to hit the water.

The tugboat-style ferry carries six cars at a time. Despite the location's isolated feel, the ferry handles one hundred or so vehicles per day. Best of all, it's free!

"Is there any food aboard the ferry?" I asked the kind ferry operator girl.

"Um, no. It's like a five-minute trip," she replied.

"Oh. How about a movie?"

"No. Look, it's less than five minutes. It's like three minutes."

"Oh. Can I get out and walk around?"

"We'd prefer you didn't."

"Well . . . can I fish?"

"No, it's not allowed," she said impatiently.

"Okay, fine, I guess I'll just sit and enjoy the cruise."

"It's not a cruise," she said.

"It is if you live in Alberta," I replied.

Despite the lack of onboard entertainment and services, it was a pleasant ride, and she really was a very helpful and friendly girl. Although she did look at me rather strangely when the ride ended and I told her I wanted to go back to the side I'd just come from.

"But it's free!" I protested. "Can't I ride back and forth as many times as I want?"

"I don't know," she said. "No one's ever wanted to do that before."

After the cruise ended (I only made her cross the river fourteen times), I headed back up through the river valley, stopping momentarily at a historical site commemorating a location where Alexander Mackenzie overwintered one year. Alex obviously had impeccable taste.

By nightfall I pulled into "The Land of 12-Foot Davis." Peace River is, as one would anticipate, situated on the bank of the Peace River in a truly picturesque setting. It's the biggest town in these parts by far, weighing in with 6,200 or so peace-loving souls.

A municipal park along the waterfront was home to the legendary 12-Foot Davis, or at least, to a statue resembling the pioneer. I'm not sure if he really was 12 feet tall, but certainly this Davis character seems to have had a rather massive heart. An interpretive sign informed me that Davis was "a friend to everybody" and that "he never locked his door." Davis probably never made it to Surrey.

?

I woke up to a cloudless sky, a particularly beautiful thing in northern Alberta. What is it that makes the sky seem bigger here than in the south? Maybe it's an optical illusion? Or maybe it's because the spaces seem even more expansive and lonely up here. Or maybe, just maybe, it's because I hadn't had a cup of coffee yet.

Fueling up at a local coffee shop, I backtracked to Grimshaw, "Mile Zero on the Mackenzie Highway," which I had missed by taking the valley route into Peace River.

Despite its sombre-sounding name, Grimshaw is a very pleasant town, the perfect launching site for a journey northward. The Mackenzie Highway opened in 1950, and civic leaders from Grimshaw had lobbied hard to be "mile zero" along the highway. Grimshaw was first known as "The Stop," probably because people stopped there a lot (duh), before making the 465-kilometre trek northward to the Northwest Territories border.

I popped into the information trailer, where I met Jeannie and Carmen—the two friendliest information attendants I encountered in all of my Alberta travels. (If everyone was this friendly, I'd venture to say there would be a lot less road rage on the highways.)

"The Americans stop in on their way north. The Canadians are all headed south," Jeannie told me.

"Sounds typical," I said, nodding sagely, as though this is what I'd expected. "Do you get any silly questions?"

"Do you drive a dogsled?"

"No, why?" I replied.

"No," Carmen said, "that's one of our silly questions we've been asked. And 'Do you live in igloos?'"

"Are these the folks heading south asking those questions?" I asked.

"Hey, we've got another one to add to our list!" Jeannie replied.

They bestowed a Mackenzie Highway pin upon me—it featured the highway distances in miles.

"We're rebels up north," they confided. "Plus, the Americans can't do metric."

At their urging, I scanned the guest book. A Red Deer traveller had written "Boy, did we make a wrong turn!" Another comment mysteriously read "Tombstone head placement." Was this a code for something nefarious? There were numerous entries from assorted Americans on the way to Alaska, and, I was pleased to see, lots of notations from southern Albertans.

Before leaving, I asked my standard question, one I'd posed to many locals on my Alberta travels: "Is there anything wacky or amusing about Grimshaw?"

As so many before her have responded, Carmen (or it might have been Jeannie . . . I think I've mixed them up now), with a look of grim intensity, replied, "I've lived here all my life. Nothing wacky ever happens here."

I headed north along Mackenzie Highway for an hour or so to get a taste of the countryside before turning south. There was now a mix of coniferous and deciduous trees, rolling parkland, and lots of llamas. I considered taking a side trip to the exotic bird museum in Deadwood (suggested town slogan: "Home of the Bureaucrat"), but realized it was too early for the museum to be open.

There was a traffic sign along the highway offering this helpful bit of advice: "No Passing When Traffic Approaching." Thank the Lord for insightful signs like these. I can't imagine what would be going on up here without them.

A giant moose statue welcomed me to Manning: "The Land of the Mighty Moose." If they really wanted to draw in tourists, I suggested to a local, they should add a statue of Preston Manning sitting on the moose with antlers on his head. (Why do people scurry away so quickly whenever I make a simple suggestion? I'm just trying to be helpful.)

Manning is also home to a truck museum, which makes at least three truck museums I've encountered in the province. We really do like our trucks in Alberta. Groovy, baby.

(Are you enjoying my random and haphazard inclusion of these retro terms? I'm trying to convey the emotional impact of my Peace and Love Tour.)

Although the north was calling me toward her expansive bosom, I needed to turn around and return to my circle trip through the Peace.

South along Highway 2, past the village of Nampa, which didn't have a town slogan. It concerns me a little when towns are slogan-less—I fear these communities are lacking a sense of direction or destiny.

Shortly after Nampa, "The Little Community with the Heart of a Happy Woodsman" (okay, I'll keep working on the slogan), I left Highway 2 for a secondary route that would take me through the communities of Marie Reine, Jean Cote, and Girouxville. You may have noticed that these place names sound very, how would you say it, French. Sure enough, these towns truly were petite French enclaves, with bilingual or even (gasp!) unilingual French signs on some buildings. In fact, nearly all the tombstones in the Girouxville cemetery seemed to display French names! Right here in Alberta! Mon Dieu!

There were no people visible in these communities, but there were lots of sheep, presumably bilingual or even French sheep, because I heard several of them bleating out, "La baa, la baa." (That could be the most embarrassing joke in the entire book, which is saying quite a lot, I think.)

I stopped in for a whirlwind visit through the historical museum in Girouxville, one of those great eclectic museums that has everything and anything old they could get their hands on, with no worries about keeping to a theme, unless of course, the theme was "If it's old, it's in!"

Groovy, baby. Peace, man.

Heading east along Highway 49 to Falher, another key destination on my route, owing to its dual status as the "Honey Capital of Canada" and "Home of the World's Largest Bee!" Falher is another community with a strong French presence, reflected in its bilingual welcome sign, "La Plus Gros a Belle au Monde!" (My French is a little rusty, but I think that loosely translates into "Home of the Fattest Monkey!")

With 48,000 hives in the area, Falher can legitimately lay claim to the title of honey capital of Canada, producing more than 4.5 million kilograms of honey each year. Of course, in my humble opinion, free honey samples would help cement the reputation.

A drive down Main Street took me past the Honeycomb Inn

Giant bee invades northern Alberta. Details at eleven.

and Lounge and a honey/gift shop aptly named the Bee Hive. A sign on a sandwich board in the centre of Main Street advertised "Doctor Recruitment Night." I'd have loved to have found out what sort of strange rituals happen during doctor recruitment night, but I had to press on. (But, I bet you anything the *doctors* get free honey.)

Other than the Bee Hive and the Honeycomb Inn, there was little evidence that the town had truly embraced its theme as the honey capital with the sort of enthusiasm Vulcan has embraced its *Star Trek* theme. If that were the case, I would have fully expected to see many Falher townsfolk dressed up in cute little bee costumes. But, I guess it was not meant to bee.

The world's largest bee is located in a small park along the main street. The metallic bee, which resembles something out of a 1950s sci-fi B flick, is 6.9 metres long, 2.3 metres in diameter. A sign explains its symbolism: "the industrious insect represents our community spirit well." Apparently, the metallic bee is a bit of a disappointment to some visitors, who expect to see *literally* the world's largest bee—as in, 6.9 metres of living, buzzing, stinging, ferocious, flying terror, held captive, one would presume, inside a gigantic bee hive the size of a small apartment.

East of Falher, at McLennan, I stretched my legs along a birding boardwalk that led out to Kimiwan Lake, a major staging area for waterfowl. I sat for a few moments and watched a group of dabbling ducks do their thing, which is basically dabble, hence the term "dabbling ducks."

At some point, six ducks formed a perfect circle, then, in perfect unison, all dunked their heads at the same time, thrusting their feathered rumps high into the air. Finally, after all these years, it dawned on me what the inspiration for synchronized swimming had to have been.

I popped on over to High Prairie for lunch, and on the way back east to Grande Prairie, noticed a sign with a map of the four western provinces that read "Independence is the answer." Being a fan of the game show *Jeopardy*, I tried my best to respond to the answer in the form of a question:

"What is a really stupid way to destroy the greatest country on the planet?"

or

"What is the least effective, costliest, and stupidest way to get Ottawa off our backs?"

or perhaps

"What is . . . are you freaking insane?"

This sign, like others around the province invites Albertans to rally around the idea of forming our own little nation of Albertania (we'd have to change our name). To supplement the signs, there are even Web sites dedicated to Alberta's separation. In fact, the aspiring Albertan separatist can even purchase "Republic of Alberta" thongs off the Internet, because nothing makes for a more striking political statement than a thong.

I don't know about you (I'd really *like* to know about you, but simple mathematics makes it impossible), but this notion of Alberta separation cracks me up. I mean, haven't you been reading my book? This is one cool place, full of gophers, great-smelling people, and giant food items. We are blessed with so much in Alberta, why go looking for more?

Of course, Albertans aren't the only ones. It seems more and more Canadians, from BC to Newfoundland, are feeling alienated from Ottawa. So I think there is only one solution to the regional disparities faced in this country, only one solution that will make everyone uniformly happy, only one solution that a *real* Albertan could come up with: Ontario must leave the country.

There it is. The one solution that will work for everyone. Ontario, as the only region of Canada that doesn't feel misunderstood by, well, Ontario, is the province that needs to separate in order to make everyone else feel better about their lot in Canada.

Let's face it, it's a win-win situation. I mean, how can Ontario complain about becoming a country? They already think they're the centre of everything, so let's just make it official. Just imagine, no more Ottawa! No more Toronto Maple Leafs! No more Toronto! Please, help me kick-start a movement by embracing my exciting, brand-spanking-new party—the "Ontario Must Leave in Order to Save the Rest of Canada" Party!

But I digress.

The gorgeous river valley at Smoky River has snapped me back to the here and now. With scenery like this, who the hell needs to worry about separation? Peace, my fellow Albertans, peace and love.

My whirlwind Peace and Love tour was drawing to a close as I pulled into Grande Prairie.

Although Fairview is the "Heart of the Peace," and Hay River is the "Hub of the North," and Valleyview is the "Portal of the Peace," Grande Prairie is obviously the business capital and booming centre of the Peace. More than forty thousand folks call Grande Prairie home, and the hotels and motels are often filled to the brim with oil field workers from around the region. Like Fort McMurray, this is a city that shows no signs of slowing down and every sign of being in a permanent state of boom-ness.

My taxi driver, the one who got lost in the fog at the trip's start, told me Grande Prairie was experiencing such incredible growth that every time he turned around, and I quote, "there was someone new in my cab!"

I paid a visit to the Grande Prairie Visitor Centre and Museum. For three dollars, you can tour some impressive exhibits delving into the Peace Country region. The "Three Bs of the Peace" are highlighted in the museum: bison, bees, and berries. Here you can learn, for example, that one-third of all bison in Alberta is produced in the Peace, that 40 percent of all the beehives in Canada are here, and that berry producers represent a $75-million industry.

A wonderful display features a robotic dinosaur (Grande Prairie was home to a major dinosaur discovery in the 1970s that has prompted a bit of a northern dino bone rush) that moves its eyes and head now and then—just enough to freak you out a little. Another display features a model of a Pleistocene horse, which clearly must have been the inspiration for the Mohawk haircut. For something a little gruesome, there's the story of an RCMP officer who had to chop the head off a frozen murder victim so that he could haul the evidence back home for further investigation. Isn't history romantic?

By far my favourite part of the museum was the outhouse display, featuring an actual outhouse. (Any museum that includes an outhouse gets major points from me.) There's also mention of a 1917 Grande Prairie bylaw stipulating that outhouses had to be built at the farthest end of the lot, and that the cleaning and emptying of outhouse contents had to be done in as inoffensive manner as possible. The display reminds us of the importance of the outhouse: "Frigid in the winter and smelly in the summer the outhouse was one of the earliest settlements built on homesteads." Inside the outhouse, on the seat, was my favourite outhouse quote, from Donald Cameron, author of *Outhouses of the West*: "The western outhouse was symbolically the seat of government. The place where the equality of all people was perceptible." Well said.

My last stop in the museum and, fittingly, my last stop on my Peace and Love Tour was at an exhibit featuring, once again, big-hearted 12-Foot Davis, whose real name was Henry Fuller "12-Foot" Davis. A quote attributed to him, dated August 1900, nicely summed up the theme of my tour:

"I never killed nobody,
I never stole from nobody,
I never wilfully harmed nobody,
And I always kept an open house for all travellers all my life.
No miss, I ain't afraid to die."

I thought about this quote as I stepped out into the bright blue sunshine and into a blustering Peace Country wind.

Of course 12-Foot Davis wasn't afraid to die. He didn't have to catch a plane back to Calgary.

Peace, baby. Peace and love.

"12-Foot Davis" also known as "3.6576-Metre Davis."

An Albertan and an Ontarian are talking in a bar. The Albertan asks the Ontarian what he would be if he weren't an Ontarian.

"Hmmm, I've always liked BC, so I guess I'd become a BCer. How about you? If you weren't an Albertan, what would you be?"

"Embarrassed," the Albertan replies.

tips for the travelling albertan

From time to time, Albertans may find it necessary to leave the safe confines of their rat-free, PST-free, debt-free province. The choice to do so should be immediately reconsidered, however if you are still intent on heading out into the world, here are a few helpful tips.

When travelling in Saskatchewan
- Never ask them about daylight savings time, this will only stress them out.

- Never, under any circumstances, slip up and reveal anything about our plans to take over their province.

- Just nod your head vigorously when they suggest that the Saskatchewan Roughriders are Canada's team and then back slowly out of the room. If necessary, play dead.

- Always carry wallet-sized photos of the Rockies with you. They'll enjoy seeing what mountains look like.

When travelling in BC
- When parking your car, always straddle the parking line a little to let them know you're there.

- They seem to enjoy it when you drive really, really close behind them.

- If they mention the beautiful ocean scenery on the coast,

change the conversation by asking them how much PST they paid on their last car purchase.

- It's always a fun icebreaker to ask them if Vancouver is going to get a real hockey team any time soon.

When travelling in Manitoba
- Yeah, right, like anyone's going to travel to Manitoba.

When travelling to Ontario
- Never ask them if they still have lots of "bums and creeps."

- Try to minimize your shock when you gas up a vehicle (we don't want them thinking we're too well off).

- Heck, you might as well ask if they're getting a real hockey team soon, too.

When travelling to Quebec
- Never, ever say, "When are you Frenchies getting the hell out?" (This only upsets them, as I discovered the first time I met my in-laws.)

- Never ask if you are still in Canada.

- Don't speak louder in an attempt to communicate with French-speaking Quebecers, unless they appear to be quite old.

When travelling in the Maritimes
- Never say, "So what's the big deal with Anne of Green Gables, anyway?"

- If they start droning on about seafood, offer them a prairie oyster.

- Never remind them that Alberta could purchase all three Maritime provinces *and* still have money left over to take everyone to Disneyland.

When travelling to Newfoundland

- Never say, "What language are you speaking?"

- Never ask if you are still in Canada.

- If they mention the great ocean scenery, change the conversation by asking them how much PST they paid on their last car purchase.

When travelling in Texas

- Try to casually throw the Canadian Rockies, our gargantuan cows, and our bottomless oil wells into the conversation at every opportunity, even if people are speaking about linen.

- When visiting a ranch, always look around confused and say, "Well, this must be the *guest* ranch, where's the real one?"

- To help build instant rapport, try this line: "Wow, you're just like us only without the gorgeous scenery and friendly people!"

When travelling in France

- Never ask a local how many barrels the Eiffel Tower produces.

- Never say, "Aren't you the same people whose asses we kicked on the Plains of Abraham?"

When travelling in South America

- Never drink the water (this is just good advice for anyone, really).

There you have it. I don't have time to get into other destinations, but I hope these tips help you with your future travels. And if they don't, well, like I said, you should have stayed home anyway.

why canada needs more alberta

Alberta. So much to give . . . so little time . . .

Canada is in trouble. Deep trouble. One need only look at Peter Mansbridge's receding hairline to appreciate just how far off the rails we've gone.

There's only one province with the wherewithal, talent, gorgeous looks, entrepreneurial spirit, charm, and cash in hand capable of saving the country. Yes, it's little old us—Alberta, saviours of this great nation.

I'm sure the rest of Canada wants to know how I plan to save the country, so here's my simple step-by-step plan, inspired by Alberta:

Create more giant roadside attractions.

If you've ever driven through northern Ontario, or for that matter, many parts of Canada that I'm too polite to name, you can clearly see that Canada is in dire need of more roadside attractions. It doesn't matter what, anything, *please*. For God's sake, just give us something to look at!

With Alberta's expertise in this field, we could easily help northern Ontario plan the World's Largest Piece of Dental Floss or the World's Biggest Briquette or the Longest Toothpick. (These are just examples. For all I know, they are already taken. Not to worry, we'll work out the details.)

Eradicate the country of rats, starting with Toronto.

We've effectively firewalled the rats out of our own province—no reason to think we can't tackle Toronto rats next. Sure it could be a little ugly, a little messy, but over the long run you'll be glad we helped. (This will do more to bring business to Toronto than any stinkin' Rolling Stones concert could ever hope to achieve.)

Build a cultural bridge between Quebec and Texas.

Albertans are very chummy with Texans, and we have a lot in common with Texas, so Alberta can easily function as a bit of a cultural matchmaker by bringing these fine people together and building some important bridges. Chili poutine, anyone?

Build more Plus 15s.

The rest of Canada, save parts of British Columbia, is far too cold in the winter for most normal people to function properly. Alberta can go a long way toward solving this problem by constructing a vast network of Plus 15–covered walkways throughout the prairies, eastern Canada, the Maritimes, and especially Newfoundland. In fact, with a little Alberta ingenuity, there's no reason not to have a Plus 15 all the way from Nova Scotia to Newfoundland.

Break down the tension between the Feds and Quebec.

No one knows how to get along with the federal government better than Alberta. We can teach Quebec the subtle art of persuasion when it comes to negotiating with the Feds, like no one else can. And by introducing Quebec to our giant sausage and pyrogy, we can easily persuade Quebec to drop this whole nonsense about being a "distinct society."

Create a truly bilingual nation.
Nothing sounds more pathetic than an eastern politician trying to yell "Yahoo!" during the Calgary Stampede. With some western language skills training, the rest of Canada could become fully bilingual in a surprisingly short time.

Replace Anne of Green Gables' house with an annex of West Edmonton Mall.
This Anne of Green Gables thing is surely going to slow down soon. I think now is the time for the Maritimes to begin planning for the future, a future, sadly, that doesn't include Anne and her little dog. (Does she even have a little dog?)

The perfect solution is to build a 3-million-square-foot (roughly half the size of PEI) West Edmonton Mall II complex. Sure, calling it West Edmonton Mall II may seem odd at first, but this will pass, because when those cash registers start chiming, folks will soon be saying, "Anne who?"

Teach the rest of Canada how to properly manage its finances.
Some people argue that Alberta is just lucky. That it's only owing to a fluke of geography that we enjoy the spectacular scenery of the Rockies and the wealth produced through oil revenues. These people would be non-Albertans. Because real Albertans know that we are also hard-working, driven, entrepreneurial folks who know how to manage our money.

So with our financial acumen, it won't be long before Canada says goodbye to its ongoing financial drains such as the despised GST, the federal debt, or health, social, and education services. With our simple plan (as seen first on *Dr. Phil*), we can have the rest of Canada on the fast track to wealth, success, and untold riches.

The entire plan shouldn't take more than three years, tops, to implement. As for the costs, well, let's not worry about these things right now, okay? The important thing is that Canada needs saving, and Alberta is up to the task.

You're welcome.

about fifth house

F ifth House Publishers, a Fitzhenry & Whiteside company, is a proudly western-Canadian press. Our publishing specialty is non-fiction as we believe that every community must possess a positive understanding of its worth and place if it is to remain vital and progressive. Fifth House is committed to "bringing the West to the rest" by publishing approximately twenty books a year about the land and people who make this region unique. Our books are selected for their quality, saleability, and contribution to the understanding of western-Canadian (and Canadian) history, culture, and environment.

Look for the following titles from Fifth House at your local bookstore:

Aunt Mary in the Granary and Other Prairie Stories,
    by Eileen Comstock
The Canadian Rockies Guide to Wildlife Watching,
    by Michael Kerr
Cold as a Bay Street Banker's Heart: The Ultimate Prairie
    Phrasebook, by Chris Thain
Don't Name the Ducks and Other Truths about Life in the
    Country, by Wendy Dudley
The Hudson's Bay Boy: From Cabbagetown to Rupert's Land,
    by John Seagrave
In Grandma's Kitchen, by Eileen Comstock
No Spring Chicken: Thoughts on a Life Well Lived,
    by Eileen Comstock
Prairie Memories, by Eileen Comstock
Sunny Side Up: Fond Memories of Prairie Life in the 1930s,
    by Eileen Comstock
When Do You Let the Animals Out? by Michael Kerr